ADHD RAISING AN EXPLOSIVE CHILD

LOIS BAXTER

CONTENTS

INTRODUCTION

"The emotion that can break your heart is sometimes the very one that heals it..."

— NICHOLAS SPARKS

It can be heartbreaking when you first find out your child has Attention Deficit Hyperactivity Disorder. You might feel confused, ashamed, or angry. You know your child has some difficulties, but maybe you never imagined they would have a label for those difficulties. When you learn more about this condition, you start to see more areas of struggle. Your family might feel like it's turning upside down until you look at the child in front of you. Your son or daughter might have a new label, a new reason for all of the fidgeting and fighting. But your child is still the same person they have been all along. The early days of seeking a diagnosis and receiving one are tough stuff.

As a parent of children with ADHD myself, I can tell you that *you* are also made of stern stuff. You are a parent that has to add a few little badges to that parent one you carry because you are also a coach, a referee, a de-escalation expert, a chef, a taxi driver, a meditation guru, and a negotiator. Of course, you might be thinking, "I'm really just a parent," but when there's ADHD in your household, you will be wearing multiple hats every day!

Throughout the coming chapters, we are going to dive into the common issues seen in ADHD. Of course, ADHD affects each person differently, and the level of support a person has determines how the symptoms are expressed to a certain extent. We will look into the 80/20 rule, which states that if you can manage 20 percent of the symptoms, you'll see results in about 80 percent of the person's life. Not only that but, we are also going to be looking into self-care and what to do when you aren't sure about medicating your child. We aren't shying away from any of the hard conversations and you will have space to reflect on the situation at hand for you.

If you want to make a note of where you're at right now in the ADHD journey, and where you would like to be, go ahead. You might find that you are 10 steps closer after reading this book. My goal with this book is to help you see that you are already doing a great job, and to provide you with some key information on the topic of ADHD so you feel better equipped to deal with it at home, in your classroom, in your family, and wherever else you need to.

ADHD is a complex condition and it brings a host of complex social, emotional, and psychological issues. That being said, these are things that can be managed with the right information and a kind approach. ADHD does not define a person.

Maybe you are looking for some information about ADHD because you'd like to be able to support a family member with ADHD a little better. Perhaps you're an adult with ADHD and you want to know how you might parent a child with the condition.

Whatever your background, you'll have a host of new ideas to help you out. You'll learn about:

- The different types of ADHD.
- Identifying triggers in the environment
- How ADHD causes explosive behavior
- The beauty of the ADHD brain
- How to manage expectations of yourself and your child
- The societal views of ADHD
- Self-care for parents
- Bullying
- Social exclusion
- Sleeping issues
- The pros and cons of medication
- The benefits of ADHD

And a whole lot more. The only thing you need to do is give yourself the time to settle into the information I've got for you, and go easy on yourself. I'm a huge fan of being gentle with myself. The world is hard enough, why add self-criticism to life?

You are ready for the next step in the ADHD journey. So, settle in, and let's begin.

1

ADHD AND ME

"You can't change who you are, and you shouldn't be asked to."

— JONATHON MOONEY

W hen you have a baby, you probably never dreamt that one day you would be bringing your child to a doctor or psychologist for parenting advice. You probably didn't think that your little bundle of joy would ever cause you so much confusion, or that there would be so many trips to the school. Let's be honest here, having children is an experience no one can prepare you for.

And add in a diagnosis of ADHD, and you just feel like the parenting playbook has been tossed out the window.

Before we go any further, it's good to acknowledge that no one really wants to feel like there's a label on their child. We don't like to think there's any kind of issue or 'disorder' because it implies there's something *wrong*. But that's not where we're working from in this book. We are accepting the fact that ADHD is just an outward expression of your child's brain wiring. And sometimes this outward expression is tough to deal with as a parent. You might have felt relieved when there was an official name on the ADHD behavior, but it's okay if you felt a little sadness too.

But since you're here, I'm betting you know that ADHD can be a real gift. Sure, it can be challenging but it's a part of your child. It's built into their personality and you are okay with that. The main focus now is understanding ADHD, how it impacts your child, and practical ways of supporting your child so they can feel happy and calm. If we can support a person whose brain is wired that bit differently, we can help them reach their full potential with minimal explosions along the way.

In this chapter, we are going to dive into the background of ADHD. We will look at how it differs from Attention Deficit Disorder (ADD), the types of ADHD, and the symptoms you will see. We'll also look at why a child with ADHD might 'explode' and what you can do about it. As a parent of three beautiful children, I can confidently tell you that each child is unique. Even if two children have the same label on paper, they will look different in reality. This is vital to remember. Of course, we might forget this but it might be a clue as to why there's so much frustration for both child and parent.

DEFINING ADHD

ADHD, Attention Deficit Hyperactivity Disorder, is a common neurodevelopmental disorder. It is most often discovered and diagnosed in childhood and it lasts into adulthood. The person diagnosed with ADHD might be inattentive, hyperactive, impulsive, and have difficulty getting along with other people. ADHD can be difficult to see at first because some of the signs and symptoms are common in children. For instance, if your child talks a lot and loves running around at any opportunity, this doesn't necessarily mean they have ADHD. But if you see your child struggling with decision-making, getting into numerous fights with peers, and struggling with their emotions on a daily basis, then investigating the source is a logical step to take.

Children with ADHD don't grow out of the behaviors the way their peers do. The tantrums you see in a three-year-old might still happen for the eight-year-old who has ADHD. A child with ADHD might lose their things multiple times a day when their non-ADHD friends don't. This child might also move nonstop or talk over others without even noticing. There are a lot of children who talk a lot with ADHD, but there are some children who have more of an issue in waiting for their turn in talking. This can obviously cause frustration and it's a noticeable trait in ADHD.

At the root of ADHD, there is a brain difference. This means that a person without ADHD operates in a way that is deemed 'typical' by society. But a person with a brain that is wired slightly differently will behave in a way that might seem a little different than what is expected.

How does it develop? Well, no one knows for sure. There is a ton of research on what might contribute to a person developing ADHD but the reality is that there seems to be many factors at play and not one specific root cause. As a parent, it can seem like a sea of *what-ifs* but that self-blame needs to be left aside! ADHD can happen in any family and there's no research to tell you what you can do to prevent it.

That being said, genetics seem to play a role in whether or not a person develops ADHD and this is something that is completely out of our hands. We can't control our genetics. It's just the luck of the draw! That might sound harsh but it's the truth. Just like we don't know what color eyes or hair we'll get, we have no idea what kind of brain we will have either. Aside from genetics, research shows that there are a few other correlated factors in developing ADHD.

These include:

- Low birth weight or a premature delivery
- Exposure to major toxins in the environment during the pregnancy
- Brain injury

As you can see, these are also things that we cannot control. Oftentimes people don't know if there are toxins in their environment. Likewise, people cannot control the birth weight of a baby and premature delivery is rarely expected or planned. You can see that you would exhaust yourself as a parent, trying to figure out what might have caused ADHD in your child. The fact is it's there and now we need to figure out what to do about it!

Just like every person is different, every diagnosis can look different. Each person with ADHD will find it impacts them slightly differently. On the outside, two people with ADHD can look and behave very differently too. So what are the different types? The American Psychological Association has identified three different types of ADHD and this is really helpful to know.

You might have read about ADHD in the past and thought, "well, that doesn't sound like my little Jack," and that's good information to have as a parent. Trust your gut when it comes to your little ones. So when you read this next part, keep in mind that not every child fits neatly into a category. Your experience is unique to you and your family. Let's take a look at the different types.

Types of ADHD

Each type of ADHD looks different and will have a different treatment. The first subtype is known as the Inattentive Type. This has a list of nine symptoms and for most people, there will be around six or seven symptoms present. For a person to fit into this subtype of ADHD, they will not really have any of the symptoms that go along with the next subtype.

So what are the symptoms you might see with the inattentive type?

- First off, you might notice a high number of careless mistakes. An example might be a child leaving their drink close to the edge on tables, countertops, and basically anywhere they set it down. Even though their drink might tip over and spill time and time again, they might continue to make the same mistake the next time. Another example might be forgetting to roll up their sleeves when they wash their hands. When this happens throughout the day, the child might be really uncomfortable because their arms are feeling wet. These are small examples but the mistakes can build up and make a day feel stressful for a child. A lot of careless mistakes are easy to notice and there can be teasing from others after a while. This isn't meant to stress you out as a parent, but it's good to get some insight into how your child might be feeling when things are building up.

- The second symptom is not paying attention to detail. This can be a big problem when it comes to things like school assignments. If you can imagine that your child comes home crying and when you ask what's wrong they reply that they failed another test. After a bit of discussion, you realize they didn't fail because they had gotten the answers wrong. Rather, they had failed because they hadn't read the right question and so their test was completely off track. This is so disheartening for a child and it can be distressing if it happens multiple times. Another example might be wearing clothes backward or inside out. Listen, we all do this sometimes! But for a child with ADHD, this can be a daily occurrence, even when they are past the preschool stage.

- Another symptom of inattentive ADHD is having trouble paying attention and sticking to a task. This can cause arguments and disruption at school or even at home. If a child has to be reminded 10 times to do something, then eventually the adult might feel as though the child is purposefully moving away from the chore or given task. If you are that adult doing all of the remindings, try to keep this point in mind!

- Similar to the previous symptom, a person with ADHD might struggle to listen. They might hear the first half of a sentence but the second half has evaporated. As a result, the communication can get a little sticky between a person with ADHD and a person without this diagnosis.

- People with ADHD have a hard time being able to follow and understand instructions. They might need something broken down into steps and then written down. For example, you might see that your child has difficulty getting ready for school in the mornings. When you wake her up and say it's time to get ready, she might be able to dress herself, get her school bag ready, make her own breakfast, brush her hair and teeth —the whole lot! But putting all of these steps together might be an issue. She might get through the breakfast and hygiene part of the morning alright. But the school bag is left to the side and your child is getting frazzled, wondering what to do next. Leaving her to do it all on her own would mean that her lunch gets left behind and no one makes it out of the door on time. This doesn't mean that you need to do everything for your child, but it does mean support techniques need to be implemented so your child can feel secure in her routine. If she forgets the steps in her day, you're there to help.

- Some individuals with ADHD will do anything in their power to avoid tasks that involve effort. They just do not have enough internal resources to get this activity done and they would rather turn away from it. Again this can be problematic because there are so many daily tasks that involve effort.

- The inattentive ADHD type often means the person is distractible and forgetful. These are technically separate symptoms but they overlap quite a bit. After all, when we get distracted then we often forget what it was we were distracted from! Imagine a child who struggles with staying on task. This child finds it difficult to follow instructions but they are trying their best. All seems to be going well when all of a sudden, a loud noise comes from the other room. This child gets completely distracted from their task and is now having a hard time remembering what they had been doing and why it was important. This is a cycle that can quickly become exhausting for the child.

- The final symptom for the inattentive subtype is losing things necessary to complete a task.

As you can imagine, and probably know very well, these symptoms can be incredibly anxiety-provoking and frustrating for a child with ADHD. As a parent, you can feel powerless in situations where your child is frustrated or overwhelmed because it's difficult to know how to help. But you're trying your best! We'll look at techniques you can use later on.

For now, let's look at the next subtype of ADHD. The next subtype is known as the HyperActive Inattentive type. To be diagnosed with this, a child usually has six or more of the symptoms and they do not usually have many of the Inattentive type symptoms.

- Fidgeting and squirming are common in this type of ADHD. Sometimes the child might seem like their hands and their feet cannot stop moving. They might be the child zipping around with a seemingly endless pool of energy. This can be a difficulty because there are many situations where we are required to sit still. These children need frequent movement breaks so they can move their bodies and not feel constrained.

- A related symptom is getting up when seated. From the outside, it almost looks like the child has ants in his pants! He cannot sit for as long as his peers and this can be distracting in situations such as school, or waiting rooms.

- Running and climbing at inappropriate times is considered another symptom of this subtype of ADHD. Now, you might be thinking that most children run when they aren't supposed to and that's very true. However, for a child with ADHD, it seems like they must run. They cannot go slowly even when they've been cautioned umpteen times. Their bodies have an energy that needs to be released and so they move and run and climb and everything in between!

- Talking over others, interrupting, and blurting out unfiltered comments. This can be a difficult issue because most conversations require waiting for our turn to speak. Some parents would say that their child does not ever mean to speak over other people and the child might feel quite upset at being unable to control it. A child with ADHD might say a couple of things before they've realized what they've even said. This can cause embarrassment and disagreements.

- Another symptom is behaving as though they have a built-in battery or motor. The person with ADHD might be moving faster for longer than their peers and this can be a real strength. At the same time, the person might struggle to slow down enough to hear

what's happening around them and they
might be jumping ahead and missing out.
This element of ADHD means that the child
can struggle to relate to others who do not
have ADHD.

You might have read these lists and recognized a lot
of these symptoms. In fact, you might have read
through these lists and thought, *My child kind of fits
in both of these categories,* and that's absolutely fine! In
reality, a lot of people with ADHD have some traits
from both the Inattentive and Hyperactive Inattentive types. When a person has symptoms from both,
they are considered to fit under the Combined
subtype.

Each person is unique and the traits listed will
impact them to a different extent. You might find
that your child has five from each list but there's
only one trait or symptom that really causes a lot of
problems. It's subjective and it's less important to
know what the symptoms are, and more important
that you know how to manage them!

Before moving on, we need to look at Attention
Deficit Disorder (ADD) and how that might overlap
and differ from ADHD. In some families, there

might be a few individuals that have one or the other and it's good to know the difference.

ADD is often mistaken for ADHD. A person with ADD will have excessive attention difficulties but they will not have the impulsiveness or hyperactivity that accompanies ADHD. They will struggle with instructions in a similar way but they will not necessarily find it difficult to sit still and they won't be as prone to careless mistakes. Children with ADD will find listening a real challenge, so the parent in the situation might find themselves repeating instructions frequently. Interestingly, girls seem to be diagnosed more with ADD and boys seem to be more likely to be diagnosed with ADHD.

Both conditions mean the child will disappear into their own thoughts for extended periods at a time. The key to understanding ADD and ADHD really lies in being able to observe your child and how the symptoms they have impacts them. It's good to know the difference between ADD and ADHD, but it's even better knowing how to manage the specific symptoms you're experiencing or witnessing.

WHY DOES MY CHILD EXPLODE? DOES ADHD CAUSE THIS?

Andrea is a six-year-old child who has recently been diagnosed with ADHD. She is happy, energetic, and loves all things Pokemon. Andrea has three siblings and she has more energy than the rest of them combined. She is doing really well in all her extracurricular activities such as kung-fu and horse-back riding. However, school is a real struggle for Andrea. Her mother Lisa is worried that Andrea's frustration will build and build until the daily tantrums become hourly explosions.

At present, Andrea will have a tantrum in the morning or right before bed. During her explosions, things get broken, there's screaming, and everyone ends up upset in one way or another. Lisa isn't sure what causes the explosions, only that they are sure to happen again tomorrow. It's an exhausting cycle for Andrea and her family. There doesn't seem to be any major stressors that Lisa can see but the tantrums are ceaseless. The family needs something to change.

Andrea is trying her best each day but her ADHD has been making life difficult. At the young age of six, Andrea probably has little insight into what is causing her tantrums. From the outside, it's really unclear as to the cause of these outbursts. But if we look at the symptoms of ADHD and the demands of each day, in a particular school, we can get closer to the issue.

Mornings require multiple steps. Each day we need to make our breakfast, get dressed, find our shoes or keys, and make sure our bag is packed for the day. Oh, don't forget to brush your teeth! Don't forget to bring your lunch. And definitely don't leave your homework on the kitchen table. It's exhausting at the best of times. Add the symptoms of ADHD and you've got a recipe for disaster. Andrea might be forgetful, easily distracted, and a seemingly poor listener. If mom doesn't remind her, Andrea might forget her lunch or her homework. Some mornings become overwhelming because Andrea is frustrated with the number of steps required of her.

A person with ADHD has difficulty regulating their emotions and when this is combined with impulsivity, there can be major fireworks. A lot of times, a child will explode because they feel dis-empowered. This means they do not have the tools to deal with what is happening. They mightn't know what to say, and they do not know what to do. This level of frustration on top of feelings of powerlessness is a recipe for explosiveness.

Children with ADHD move at a different pace than others. They can become what's called "hyper-focused" and this means they get completely engrossed in the task in front of them. This hyper-focus causes difficulty in transitioning between tasks and this is most evident in school for a large number of children. If you consider a typical school day, you might imagine doing activities like art, math, science, and sports. If a teacher were to call "time up" too soon on a task, a child with ADHD might explode in frustration. The child might be hyper-focused on the task and if it's left half-finished, this would be really difficult to process.

A child with ADHD might show anger and frustration by throwing things, shouting, opposing instructions, or leaving the room. Every child is different and their reaction will match their experience. A child who does not have any issues that come with ADHD will behave much differently in a scenario like this and the child with ADHD can internalize feelings of worthlessness.

Think about it—if you were constantly leaving tasks half-finished and then having emotional outbursts afterward, you would feel like there's something wrong with you and you could be quite negative towards yourself. Over time, you might develop a negative idea of yourself and you might mistakenly believe you were stupid. But children with ADHD are not slow, stupid, or incompetent. They need understanding and adaptive strategies to flourish.

The explosions or arguments are exhausting and upsetting. When there is little understanding of ADHD in a family, the individual with the condition might feel rejected and unwanted, as well as penalized for being a little different. The ideal situation is one in which the person with ADHD is supported enough to make less careless mistakes, and understood enough so they don't feel unwanted.

How Can I Identify Triggers in the Environment?

You're working on helping your child with their needs. You know they are trying their very best to stay calm but you also know there are environmental things that need to change so there can be more harmony in your home. So how do we identify these triggers?

Consider the last time there was an explosion in your home. Was it dinnertime? Was a friend over for a playdate? Were you trying to get to an appointment on time? Think about the circumstances, and write down the time of day as well as what was going on.

Next, consider how you were at that moment. Were you calm and completely blindsided by the explosion? Or could you sense an eruption was about to take place? Were you in a bad mood already? Try to figure out what your state of being was like ahead of the explosion.

Now, what did the explosion look like? Was your child kicking and screaming? Were other people watching? Try to focus on what happened and all the elements that slot into the picture.

How did you handle the situation? Were you calm and collected? Did you raise your voice? How did you respond to the outburst?

I know these are big questions and I don't mean to have a rapid-fire round of interrogation! This part is just for you. Don't judge your answers, just try to be as honest as you can. If you have a good idea of what happened, you'll be able to figure out what went on for your child.

It's important to know what time of day has the most amount of outbursts. Tuning into this detail can help you see any pattern of behavior that might be occurring. If you can see a pattern, you'll know that there is something that definitely needs to be tweaked. Likewise for your reaction. This is in no way a criticism of you because you are doing a fantastic job as a parent. It's good to know how you react though because sometimes our reaction can be part of the problem or at least something that escalates the situation further.

If you were your child, how would you be feeling during the explosion? On the outside, it might look like there's pure rage but often the child is feeling entirely overwhelmed. They might have had five things that bothered them prior to the incident and the explosion happened because they couldn't take one more thing. An explosion looks dramatic on the outside and it feels even more so on the inside.

If you aren't the person with your child when they explode, you might feel guilty and unhappy. The guilt might be because you don't want your child to explode around another person, and it might also be because you want to be the person comforting your child. You might feel unhappy because you don't like knowing your child is having difficulties when you're not there. This is a tough part of parenting. You can't be everywhere at once so please don't beat yourself up for anything. You are doing your best and you are doing right by your child. Looking into the environment when your child has tantrums will be a useful tool in discovering what helps your child prosper and what doesn't.

To summarize what we've discussed so far, you are able to help your child by understanding them and their triggers. There are different types of ADHD and these can present like ADD. Over the coming chapters, we will get deeper into the topic of ADHD and what you can do to make life more fulfilling and straightforward for you and your child.

Here are some actionable steps you can implement, based on what we've discussed so far:

- Give your child extra time getting ready and transitioning between tasks/places.
- Help your child identify when they are reaching "explode mode." You might have a chat with emotions and when they are reaching anger/rage, that's when you can

give them extra support or extra time to become calmer.

- Set up reminders for your child so they can return to a task. You can set these reminders on your phone or even have pictures of these on the fridge.

2

THE BEAUTY OF THE BRAIN

"Your emotions make you human. Even the unpleasant ones have a purpose. Don't lock them away. If you ignore them, they just get louder and angrier."

— SABAA TAHIR

A child with ADHD is really dependent on the people around them. Every parent tries their best, but parents of children with ADHD have to be on their A-Game as much as possible. As a parent of a child with ADHD, you will face struggles on a daily basis that seem beyond belief for other parents who don't have the same experience or insight. Your greatest gift to your child is understanding them and giving yourself credit for the hard work you're doing. Good job!

Now it's time to dig into the *why* behind ADHD. As mentioned, there are a few factors that seem to be linked to ADHD development. Now it's time to look at the machine that powers your child and contributes to the wonderful, and sometimes challenging, behavior you see—The brain!

We'll also take some time to look at statistics around ADHD and how you can accept everything about ADHD, even when it feels tough.

THE BRAIN

A lot of times, we forget that behavior can be linked to an underlying health difference. We might think, "my child is hyperactive and I guess that's just how he is." We might think our child behaves whatever way they like and that's all there is to it. But it's good to remember that we are all born unique. The uniqueness of our brains impacts how we behave and how we think. Just like everyone is born looking different, no two brains are exactly the same. If we were to look deeper into this, we would reveal even more truth. How does this relate to ADHD?

Well, a person with ADHD has a different brain than a person who functions typically. For instance, a person with ADHD has a brain that produces less of the neurotransmitter norepinephrine. This is linked with dopamine and you might already know that dopamine is the feel-good hormone. Dopamine helps control the reward center in the brain and with lower levels, there will be noticeable outward struggles. You might be wondering how this translates into observable behavior and that's a great way to be thinking. One way you might notice this in your child or teen is if they have an over-dependence on screens.

Now I'm about to hate on screens or layout any judgmental information, so don't worry! The reason I mention screen time is because screens give a person a dopamine rush. Basically, screens stimulate the production of dopamine in the brain. And if you have a brain that already struggles to produce dopamine, then you would probably want to spend time doing things that trigger your reward center. Having a brain that does not produce an average amount of dopamine can really make activities like video games and movies feel incredibly pleasurable.

Research has shown that there are four areas that are impaired in an ADHD brain. This is really crucial information to have because it means we can see why a person might be trying so hard on the outside but is still struggling. Let's take a look at how these impaired areas can impact your child.

Frontal Cortex

For a person with ADHD, their frontal cortex operates in a different way. The frontal cortex is important for high-functioning activities. The frontal cortex controls attention, organization, and executive functioning. If this part of the brain is in any way impaired, a person will find it difficult to listen, plan, and organize steps in a sequence.

Does this sound familiar? We already know that a child with ADHD finds concentration and focus a near-impossible feat. Is it any wonder when we know their frontal cortex is operating completely differently than we might have expected?

Limbic System

The limbic system is located deep within the brain. This is one of the parts of the brain that is responsible for keeping us safe. The limbic gets activated when we feel threatened and we can easily get directed into a fight, flight, or freeze mode when we feel scared. If a child felt threatened by a situation, their reaction might be quite intense.

They might read a non-threatening situation as dangerous and in that case, their reaction makes sense to them. From the outside looking in, this reaction might seem bizarre or exasperating. After all, if we feel like a situation is safe, our limbic systems are not activated. But if a person feels scared or threatened on one level, then they will respond differently.

Basal Ganglia

This part of the brain is involved in inter-brain communication. The messages that go between different parts of the brain can get mixed up and can result in impulsivity. Information is not being passed on in an effective way and another result can be inattention.

Reticular Activating System

This is a relay system in the brain and it involves information coming in and exiting. When there is an issue with the reticular activating system, there will be inattention, hyperactivity, as well as impulsivity.

Considering that four parts of the brain are impaired by ADHD, it's amazing to think that a person with this neurological condition gets through their day so well. Really, it's an exhausting endeavor for a person whose brain operates differently. Life and everything therein is designed for people who do not have the issues that face a person with ADHD. So it's really amazing that you're here, making a difference by being a parent who wants to understand ADHD and all there is to it.

At its core, ADHD is considered a brain disorder. This means that you can say for certain that your child is trying their best and they aren't actively making life harder for themselves and others.

When we look at the different parts of the brain that are impacted, we can see that the following areas are all impacted:

- Social Planning and social interaction
- Judgment
- Impulsivity
- Emotional control
- Motivation
- Decision making
- Ability to delay gratification (Everything needs to happen now!)
- Time perception
- Attention (Aacap, 2017).

If you have struggles in all of these areas, then life is going to get pretty messy at times. A person with ADHD will be able to bear this mess and all it entails when they have support.

PREVALENCE OF ADHD

You might be thinking that more and more children appear to have ADHD each year. For most of us, we had no awareness of ADHD when we were young and it's only once we've become parents that we realize there are lots of children who face these difficulties.

In the United States, there are an estimated six million children diagnosed with ADHD as of 2016 (CDC, 2022). When you look at the statistics you'll see that boys are much more likely to be diagnosed with the condition and there are lots of children who will also be diagnosed with Autism Spectrum Disorder, Tourette's Syndrome, and Anxiety (CDC, 2022). The nature of ADHD means it can go in hand with other brain conditions such as those mentioned. It's unfortunate to note that almost 70% of children living with ADHD also seem to have mental, emotional, or behavioral difficulties too.

These figures can be seen on the following chart:

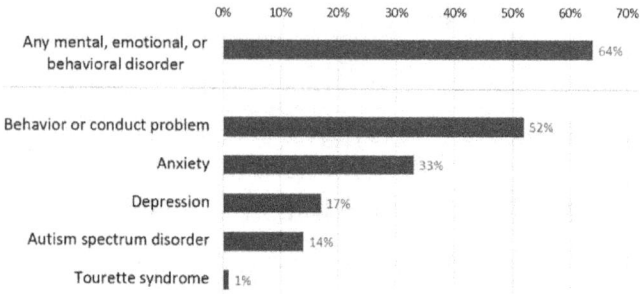

(CDC, 2022)

This graph indicates the number of children to have been diagnosed with ADHD in recent times in the United States:

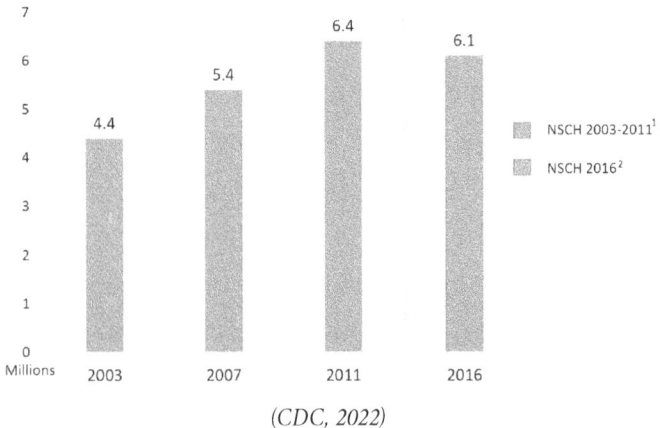

(CDC, 2022)

The estimated six million children living with ADHD represent around nine percent of all children living in the United States. The age demographic shows us that approximately 388,000 children diagnosed with ADHD are preschool age, between two and five years old. Just over two million children are aged between six and eleven, and over three million are aged 12–17.

The treatments currently offered for ADHD are a mixture of medication and behavioral therapies. When a child is aged six or under, behavioral therapy is the go-to treatment. No one seems to be trying medication as the first option for young children. As children get older, a combination of treatments seems to be the preferred approach. Almost 23% of children were receiving no formal treatment.

Each child responds differently to treatment and so you as the parent are a really wonderful asset. You know your child better than anyone and you will be able to see what is effective. You know when your child is improving and you can see what needs to be tweaked in most cases. In times when you feel overwhelmed or unsure, don't beat yourself up! You can always check with your healthcare provider for advice and there are lots of forums online where you can reach out to parents who have experienced the same things.

HOW TO ACCEPT ADHD

Whenever your child receives a diagnosis, there are bound to be mixed emotions. On one hand, you might feel relieved that the struggle is real and not just in your imagination. A diagnosis or even a discussion with a professional can be enough to validate your experiences. When you have been struggling with a child who has been exploding on a daily basis, you might be at your wit's end by the time the ADHD gets formally recognized. If you felt immediately relieved when a diagnosis was reached, then that's okay. It's always a positive experience to feel validated.

However, it is also a devastating experience to find out that your child has a label. A label that contains the word 'disorder.' This can feel like a heavy blow and as parents, we might feel grief for a while. You are not a bad parent if this sounds like you. A diagnosis brings with it new territory and your emotions might be one of these territories. You might feel angry one moment, and grateful the next.

You might be overcome with sadness and then absolutely calm that evening. There's no right or wrong way to feel. Your response towards yourself and your child is something you can control to an extent but when you are feeling a strong emotion, and you react from that place, try not to judge yourself for that reaction. The initial news that your child has ADHD can be shocking and don't forget that. Honor your emotions and don't try to minimize your internal response.

When I received the diagnosis of ADHD for my two children, it was a very different experience for both. The first time around I was in complete shock. I knew my child had a concentration issue and some impulsivity, but I did not expect my doctor to say that there might be a label for what was going on.

I wanted to reject the diagnosis and I wanted to run away. How could my child have something that might require medication and therapies? What will I do? Will I be able to manage? These were all questions running through my mind. After some time, and with a lot of support from my family, I began to pick myself back up and do my research on what to do.

The world hadn't ended, to my absolute surprise.

The second time around, I picked up my daughter's symptoms quicker. When she would have explosions, I knew that there were things in the background that might be adding up to make her feel overwhelmed. She was quite inattentive at home and I could see similarities between her and her brother. I was much more confident in how to approach the issue.

Right now my children are thriving because they have wonderful teachers, friends, and people in their lives who understand them and support them. That is my wish for every parent in a similar situation.

It's time to do a little reflection on your thoughts and experience. When you first heard the word ADHD, what was your response? Did you have any experience of ADHD when you were a child, such as a friend with the diagnosis? Did you have any notion of what a person with ADHD might need in difficult situations?

Take some time to wonder about your biases and ideas around diagnoses too. This is useful because sometimes we might not be aware of our thoughts or underlying feelings and it's always better to have a sense of what's going on under the surface. You might come to realize that actually you were relieved to have a diagnosis, a label for what has been going on. This can be so consoling because pre-diagnosis, we can feel so confused.

On the other hand, you might feel devastated by a label. You might reject it internally. This is a normal response too but in the long run, it's best to accept what's in front of you. If you need some time to be upset, that's okay. But make sure you pick yourself up when it feels right. Your child needs you and there are so many people living in a similar situation, so there is help out there.

Your child is still your little person and you are so special to them. Do what you can for both yourself and your child, and everything will be okay.

Notes for now

For a lot of parents, it's reassuring to know that there's lots of information about the ADHD brain. ADHD is prevalent among children and so, you're not alone on this parenting journey.

- Remember that your child does not process information the same way as you or their siblings might. This is helpful to know because you can amend your approach and understand what's going on for them.
- Children with ADHD have less emotional regulation which means that it takes less for an emotional outburst to spill out sometimes.

We needed to have a foundational understanding of the brain, so we can understand that the behavior is deeper than we might have initially thought. Over the coming chapters, we will discuss helpful ways of coping with the symptoms of ADHD, as well as how ADHD impacts our parenting role and expectations of children.

3

THE TERRIBLE TWOS, THREES, FOURS...

"The best inheritance a parent can give his children is a few minutes of his time each day."

— O. A. BATTISTA

When you become a parent, life takes on new meaning. Not only that but it changes from the ground up. No more lie-ins, no more free time. Okay so that's not entirely true, you still have a little time for yourself and if you don't, you need to make it a priority because self-care is essential for mental well-being.

When you become a parent, a lot is expected from you and most of it isn't easy. But when you have a child with ADHD, you need to up your game even further. You'll need to become a master at staying calm, a master at communication, and a positivity guru. That's all before nine a.m! But in all seriousness, being a parent to a child with ADHD will be difficult in a way no one can prepare you for. Your skillset as a parent needs to increase and improve.

In this chapter we're going to look at what it means to be in the parent role, understand the uniqueness of your child, and a deeper dive into why it feels like the terrible twos never end. We will also talk about the impact societal expectations can have on us and our children.

PARENTING ROLE

When a person becomes a parent, they might slip into the role with more ease than they expected. They might feel good about their actions and their parental instincts might be quite strong. For other people, it can feel more like an uphill battle from day one. Parenting is really not for the faint of heart. It's good to recognize that your ideas of parenthood, and your expectations, might be hugely different from the reality you face. That's perfectly fine! There aren't many people who would say they have had an easy run of parenting, it's just difficult by its very nature.

Let's take a look at your role as a parent. As a parent, you are the caretaker of your children. You might want to be a friend to your child but that cannot really happen until your children are adults, and even then you will still be mom or dad.

We could say that a parent is in a dual role of nurture and structure. Both are important and it's critical that we get this balance right. When a parent is in nurture mode, they are taking care of their child's basic needs. This includes food, shelter, medical needs, and clothing. The nurture mode also includes showing love, listening, paying attention, having fun, and showing an interest in their activities. When a parent is in nurture mode they are enjoying their child and showing them love and affection.

When you are nurturing, you give your child many benefits later in life. As you might know, children with positive early relationships take this on into adulthood and they have a lot of psychological bene-fits as a result of the early nurturing.

Some benefits of nurturing include:

- Your child will feel loved and loveable. They will approach the world from this mindset and this will help them to feel happier in themselves.
- A child who has been nurtured will be able to give back to others. If we do not have a nurturing upbringing, it can be really difficult to give back to others in any shape or form. Not impossible, but certainly more difficult.
- Your child will feel listened to and this is really fantastic for mental well-being. If you've ever had the experience of not being listened to, then you'll understand how important it is to feel heard.
- A child who has been nurtured will become trusting and will be an open individual.
- Your child will learn that it's okay to tackle difficult situations. When a child learns that they are loved, they become more confident and will push against difficulties. They will

THE TERRIBLE TWOS, THREES, FOURS... | 53

be okay when things don't go their way
because they have a solid base within
themselves to fall back on.

When you are a nurturing parent, you need to keep a close eye on the amount of nurture. Nurture is a positive thing but if you were to give too much, all of the time, then you might actually undo some of the benefits to an extent.

For example, if you brought your child to the playground and helped them with every slide, swing, climbing frame, or activity, you might be behaving a little overpowering. You could be overly protective and this might teach your child that they cannot trust themselves to climb on anything without you there. The goal of parenting is to really teach your child that you are there for them, but they can do it themselves.

If you were to nurture too little, then you would be emotionally distant and this can cause quite a lot of distress for a child. A child who has been nurtured too little does not learn to trust other people and may feel inadequate.

When you are in the structure mode of parenting, your role is to set a structure for your child. This includes setting limits, discipline, setting boundaries, and holding your child accountable for their actions. You also need to follow through with consequences and show them that when you say 'no,' you mean it.

When a parent sets a good structure for their child, their little one learns that rules are to be respected and that there are boundaries in place to keep them safe. We can sometimes think that boundaries and discipline must mean we are being too strict but there is a balance that needs to be struck. Being too strict won't be any better than being too lenient.

The benefits of being in structure mode mean:

- Your child feels safe and secure. They know what to expect and they know what limits are in place.
- They understand responsible behavior. This is always appropriate to their age as expecting too much or too little based on their development level will be confusing and distressing for the child.
- They feel cared for. This is down to them knowing that there are limits in place and so they know that mom or dad will always

make sure they are okay and that they are within those limits.

If there is too much structure, the child will feel inhibited and smothered. Structure mode is not about making your child follow rules, rules, and more rules: It's about having limits so everyone knows what's okay and what's not okay.

If you can offer a solid balance of nurture and structure, you will do your child an immense favor. They'll learn to trust themselves and others, and that it's okay when things go wrong. Your role as a parent is to be thoughtful, not perfect. It's actually impossible to be a perfect person, never mind a perfect parent. It's good enough to be thoughtful in your approach and balanced between discipline and affection.

Another important factor for parents to consider is consistency. It takes a lot of hard work to get consistent but it's worth it for everyone in the family. When you are consistent, your child knows what to expect. Let's take an example. Sam is an energetic child and his dad Craig is learning how to best support his son with ADHD.

On Saturdays, they go out on errands in the morning, and on the way home, they grab an ice cream. This is a lovely routine that they do most weekends and it's a real bonding experience. One Saturday, Sam gets overwhelmed and starts tantruming in the ice cream parlor. Craig is taken by surprise and tries to help Sam calm down and they return to their car. Craig bought ice cream for both of them, even though Sam had a tantrum. This might seem like a reward and for a lot of parents, their reaction would have been to leave without getting a treat.

However, in this scenario, Craig does not want to punish Sam by taking away the ice cream since he knows Sam was not tantruming in relation to the ice cream. Craig's gut feeling was to calm Sam down, do what he usually does, and try to implement discipline when there is calmness and space to do so. Craig might discipline Sam by giving him a little extra chore work to do but he won't give him a punishment that outweighs the incident.

Sam is open to doing chores as a punishment because he knows that is how Craig will lay out discipline. Sam feels understood and he knows that his dad has rules that are always there. The most important point here is that Craig is consistent and will not start punishing Sam mid-tantrum because he knows that Sam will learn more from the approach he has at present.

In this scenario, Craig offered nurture when Sam was getting overwhelmed. He also offered structure by having a consequence for the actions.

In summary, your role as a parent is to offer the support and care that your child needs. Depending on the day, there will probably be more of one or the other needed but that's okay. Striking the balance is the difficult part but something tells me you're up to the challenge.

REALISTIC EXPECTATIONS

We all have certain ideas of what is necessary for a child to learn life lessons. For example, you might remember something valuable from your childhood that you'd like to pass on to your children. And you might have some elements of your childhood packed away as things you would definitely *not* like to pass on. This is normal and we all use experiences that have shaped us to inform our parenting styles.

But since you're reading up on issues your child might be facing, you might be happy enough to challenge your old habits. You're not afraid to look at how you can improve and it's this courage that will help both you and your child flourish.

You need to set realistic expectations for yourself, and your child. This is a difficult thing to do. We often feel like superheroes and try to do everything. But the reality is that none of us are superheroes and we need to build self-care into our schedules so we can recharge our batteries when life isn't as hectic. We also can overlook the various difficulties our children face and this means we can be quite tough on them when in reality, we need to adjust our expectations of them.

I want you to consider an area of contention you have with your child. Perhaps you argue about homework and you find that you're butting heads almost every time it comes up. There could be a number of scenarios that come to mind, but I want you to focus on one recurring situation. If you can focus on one situation, try to pull apart your expectations of your child. Are you being reasonable? Is your child acting their age? Are they trying their very best? If you believe they are trying their best in that situation, why do you feel frustrated? This is a difficult thought exercise but it's worth understanding so you can feel less frustrated, and work on what you can control within the situation.

If we stuck with the homework example, we could consider the challenges facing the child. For instance, homework is a multiple-step process and this can be really tough for a child with ADHD. They might be getting overly distracted and feel like a loser because they always seem to struggle. Another thing to consider is that homework is boring most of the time! This has nothing to do with ADHD but it's good to remember because it adds a level of understanding you might not have had.

Let's say your child struggles with their homework every day, what do you think could change? Could you take movement breaks so your child doesn't feel trapped? Could you speak to their teacher and explain the difficulties? Could you do anything to prepare your child better so they can get through their homework more effectively? The answers to these questions can only be answered by you, but it's worth brainstorming. You might have felt like your child needed to do more, but as the parents, it's up to us to get creative when there's trouble. We might be expecting too much of our children without even realizing it.

You might be wondering if you've been setting unrealistic expectations unbeknownst to yourself, and how you could change that. It can feel enormous when we are faced with changing our habits. Please go easy on yourself because parenting is a difficult role. Even with amazing circumstances, parenting feels hard. Also, it's never too late to implement changes to your approach.

So, if you want to set more realistic expectations, here are some ways you can go about it:

- Ask your child how they're doing during a difficult task. Try to get an understanding of their experience and if you feel like maybe they are doing more than they can reasonably manage alone, help them simplify the task. This might include breaking the task into smaller steps and it might include you being there to shadow them during the first few simplified attempts.
- Speak to other people who have children your child's age. This can be a good way of gaining perspective on a situation. You might be feeling frustrated with your child and it might turn out that they are actually on par with their peers. Or you might find

that your child is behind their peers. Getting this information will allow you to adjust your expectations of your child.

- Allow your child to make mistakes. It's a part of life, a necessary part that we all must go through. Sure it might not be a lot of fun to be the parent in line with a child that is knocking over a display sign, but that's what children do. They knock things over, they fall, and they say things incorrectly. As long as you expect mistakes to happen, you won't be too wound up trying to make your little one perfect. Perfection does not exist in this world and that's the truth for all of us humans.

- Educate yourself as much as possible on the subject of ADHD. You're already doing this, so well done you! This is important to do because it can really help you shift your focus onto bite-size, manageable goals.

By taking action, you are doing your child and your sanity a huge favor. If you are holding your child to an unrealistic standard, the only thing that can come of it is a disappointment. It can also damage the relationship over time because a child can feel like a failure and it can take a lot of work to repair this.

But you're putting a lot of work in right now to remediate this or prevent it altogether. You can address any potential areas in your home life that might be susceptible to unrealistic expectations.

UNIQUE BEAUTY IN EACH CHILD

When we are little kids, we learn that each person is unique. And although we hear it plenty of times, it doesn't fully sink in until we're old enough to be the person saying this! But we know it's true. No two people are the same, and even two children with the same diagnosis of ADHD will look entirely different, inside and out.

Why are we talking about each person's innate uniqueness? Well, we often overlook how special our children are. This might sound shocking but it happens in the midst of real life. We get so tied up in the school runs, the dance lessons, the soccer games, the million and one things that make up our days. When we are so busy, we lose sense of the funda- mental beauty within each one of us, and each one of our children.

But I want you to just let yourself bask in the knowledge that your child, your children, are fantastic. They are unique, they are incredible, and they are yours. There's no doubt about how good they are. Take a few moments to consider the three things you love most about your child. These can be any three qualities or traits, and these are just meant for you. What I mean is, you don't need to share this exercise with your child or anyone else, unless you really want to. There are so many wonderful characteristics in each one of us, and it's lovely when we can take a moment every so often to really just sit with what we love.

Thinking about your child in this way will help you remember why you are fighting so hard to make changes. When a child is *tantruming* or getting into trouble at school, we can feel so much frustration and tiredness that we forget what we are even trying to do. Stay on track. You can get through each explosion, and each day, even if it takes a million and one tries before it feels doable. There are a lot of hard days as a parent, and this number grows when there are difficulties or issues like ADHD. But you can do it. I believe in you, and I think you ought to believe in yourself too.

Some important tips to help remember how special your child includes:

- Allowing your child to develop at their own rate. Don't compare them to other children if you can help it. Your child will do better if you can focus on their growth, their development, without bringing a non-ADHD person's development into the picture.
- Celebrate the good. If your child has yet to reach a milestone, celebrate the little steps towards that milestone. For instance, if they master a new step in their morning routine, celebrate with them. Congratulate the child on their achievement. After all, that's one more step to independence and one more badge of honor on a parent's vest.
- Your child is a unique individual and their interests will be different from yours. If you loved reading as a child, great! But it's important to remember that your child may never pick up the same pastimes as you, and that's okay. We are all different and that's what makes life interesting.

Be sure to give yourself the same compassion you are giving your child. When treating yourself well comes naturally, you'll easily be compassionate towards another person, especially your child.

SOCIETAL VIEWS OF ADHD

Have you ever been shocked by comments about your child, made by complete strangers? Or maybe a family member has said something so ignorant, and you thought you would explode? You're not alone and really, most parents experience rudeness at least once. Honestly, people offer opinions before they know it's out of their mouths. We've all been on the receiving end of rude statements, and we've all probably said something we would like to take back.

When it comes to ADHD, there is a lot of misinformation in society. When we don't understand something fully, we can be liable for getting things wrong. I want to address some of the more common misconceptions because it can be helpful to be aware of what these might be.

1. ADHD does not exist. This is false as ADHD is a recognized medical condition. Some research has also shown that ADHD can be

hereditary as about one in four people with it have a parent with ADHD. If you think back on the brain, there are actual differences that can be observed.

2. ADHD= Lazy. Ouch. That's a hard one to hear. For a person with ADHD, they might already feel like a loser when their tasks go unfinished and so this statement can be quite hurtful. People with ADHD are usually trying as hard as they possibly can.

3. Focus is just impossible for a person with ADHD. Do you remember what we talked about around hyper-focusing? A person with ADHD can have phenomenal focus at times but when they get interrupted, that's when you'll see an 'explosion.' Trying to get a person with ADHD to focus on something when they are daydreaming will seem near impossible. Yes, there are issues with focus and concentration, but it's a myth to say there's no focus at all.

4. Hyperactivity is the main symptom for all children with ADHD. This is just not true. There are a lot of children with ADHD who aren't hyperactive whatsoever. The hyperactivity that some children have is

quite remarkable and this might be why so many people think that hyperactivity is the hallmark of all ADHD cases.

5. ADHD is a disability. ADHD can certainly get in the way of learning, but it is not classed as a learning disability. If you can recall the chart we had earlier on, you might remember that there are some other conditions that co-occur with ADHD and in some instances, these might be a learning disability. But on its own, ADHD is not a disability.

6. Girls do not get ADHD. This is a tricky one because so many more boys appear to get diagnosed and their symptoms might seem more severe. However, we cannot disregard the girls who also struggle with ADHD.

7. ADHD is caused by bad parenting. Even writing this one makes me mad! This can be a tough one to encounter because it can make you, as the parent, feel so judged and so angry. If a person were to truly believe this, they would also carry enormous amounts of shame and guilt over something they've had no control over. If you hear this, or any of the others, politely tell the person

speaking that they need to check ADHD facts. These statements I'm listing can be so hurtful.

8. ADHD will go away as the person gets older. This is not true at all. A lot of adults feel like they need to hide their ADHD in the workplace for fear of judgment. But, your brain doesn't switch to neurotypicals when you hit your 18th birthday. So, it's unhelpful to think that children with ADHD don't evolve into adults with ADHD.

These views can be really tough to deal with when you have a child with ADHD. Most people do not mean harm by saying something inaccurate but as a parent, it can be a hard task to remain polite when something said makes you feel angry or frustrated.

Summing it up

You have been on quite the journey already, so well done! By reflecting on your role as a parent, you are challenging yourself to grow. By facing your expectations of your child, you are really working on making your relationship stronger so that your child will feel more supported. You might have some idea of where you need to become more nurturing, have less structure, or vice versa.

The societal views mentioned here can be really upsetting to encounter, especially when you've just found out your child has been diagnosed. But you can handle anything that comes your way, and your child is lucky to have you!

Here are some actionable steps for when you encounter misinformation around your child's diagnosis:

- Ask the other person to move on to a different topic, as you know you disagree and would like to steer clear. This is more applicable to people who aren't important in your child's life.
- Encourage family members to do some research on the topic of ADHD so they can be a good support system for you and your child.
- Share factual information where possible, and where appropriate. This might not be at the school gates, but maybe on your social media or through advocating locally for ADHD awareness.

There are a lot of areas that can become distressing in the role of an ADHD parent. But don't worry, we're going to move on to even more practical advice to help you as a parent. We still have lots of ground to cover. If you've had difficulties with sleep or anxiety, the next chapter will be a life-saver.

4

SLOWING DOWN

"Without enough sleep, we all become tall two-year-olds."

— JOJO JENSEN

I f you've ever had a child, you know that sleep disruption is a subtle form of torture. Without sleep, it sometimes feels impossible to focus, think clearly, work, communicate effectively, or motivate yourself to exercise or cook. And that's just the tip of the iceberg! When you have a child with ADHD, your day is already more complex than you may have imagined. So, it can be really hard to learn that your night will be more difficult too.

A lot of children with ADHD struggle with other issues or disorders too. This can make life quite challenging for everyone involved. Some issues that we will address alongside sleeping issues are anxiety, anger, and learning difficulties such as dyslexia. Your child has to navigate the world with their neurodivergence and you as the parent must support them along the way. This usually involves some method of slowing down enough so that your child can learn how to take care of themselves in difficult situations.

We're going to look at practical methods for doing this so both you and your child feel prepared for the situations that arise in your daily life. These techniques might be something you haven't come across before and I'm hoping you will be able to guide your child to emotional regulation so that you as the parent can also slow down, and calm down. Life can be tough, and parenting can be even tougher so we need to have helpful strategies for whatever comes our way.

USING DEFUSION TO MANAGE ANXIETY

When a person has ADHD, life is anxiety-provoking. All the details that go into our daily tasks can quickly become overwhelming. Feelings of helplessness and worthlessness can go hand in hand with anxiety too, resulting in repetitive negative thoughts. It is helpful to know what you can do about anxiety because that way you will ensure it doesn't take over either yours or your child's life.

There are so many wonderful psychotherapists and counselors out there and they have shared some awesome techniques for dealing with anxious thoughts, and I'm going to include them here. These will be helpful for you and once you have tried them yourself, you can help your child incorporate them into their well-being routines.

1. **Imagining your Mind is another Being.**
   You can look at your mind as something separate from you. You can name it anything you like or you can keep it entirely simple and just call it 'Mind.' Whenever you start having anxious thoughts, you can intervene and say internally (or out loud) *Mind, stop that,* or *Mind, that's not a helpful way of*

approaching that problem. This dialogue is really important. It shows you that your Mind is external to you and so it is something you can interact with. If you can imagine your thoughts are happening to this external being then it will be easier to interact with them. You could help your child use this by telling them to draw what their Mind looks like. If they are young, they might draw a little monster or another being. This can help them to visualize who they are speaking with.

2. **Thoughts for Sale.** We each have hundreds, thousands, of thoughts each day. You might imagine yourself having a certain budget for your thoughts and you can only use this budget for thoughts that are true. When anxious thoughts crop up, allow yourself time to inspect these thoughts. Are they true? If so, you can use some of your thought budgets on them. If they are untrue, let yourself put your thoughts aside. Imagine yourself purchasing these thoughts and placing them into your thought basket. This visualization will really make this feel more real.

3. **Keys (or pencils).** As an adult, you most probably have a set of keys that you bring with you to most places. When you have your keys, allow yourself to assign your most common anxious thoughts to each of your keys. This will help you to interact with the thought on a frequent basis so you can notice that you are carrying the thought with you, even when you might not be actively thinking about it. Your child might find that doing this with their pencils at school might work well. Externalizing the thought so you can observe it away from yourself is the main goal with each of these defusion techniques.

4. **Bully Mode.** Sometimes your anxious thoughts get super loud and aggressive, and they can really behave similarly to a bully. If you really focus on a common anxious thought you've been having, you'll see that it can be rude and it just barges in at the most inconvenient times. Treat it like the bully it is! You can speak to it and say things like, *You're not the boss here, you're just a thought.* There are lots of things you can say to it and it would be amazing if you could get it to

quiet down for long enough so you can carry out whatever you need to do.

5. **A Noisy Radio.** This technique involves imagining you are sitting in a car with a radio on full blast. The anxious thoughts are getting louder and louder and it can almost feel unbearably loud. But you can reach forward and turn the volume down. All it takes is a little effort and there's silence. With a moment's silence, you have some space to gather your internal strength, and when the radio comes back on, you will have the energy to face it and turn it down again.

6. **Silly Voice.** This is a really great technique for a person of any age. When you have a distressing thought, repeat it back to yourself using a silly voice. It can be a character's voice or just a goofy one you've made up. This will help you to hear a thought in a new light and it will take the edge off the anxiety.

When you use techniques like these, you are essentially gaining some space from your anxiety. These suggestions are known as "defusion techniques." These techniques are valuable in the treatment of anxiety because we cannot really manage our anxiety when it feels like it is taking over our minds and our bodies. Anxiety is a common experience for most people with ADHD so it's really important to know how to deal with it when it crops up!

GETTING THE BALANCE RIGHT FOR SLEEP

For many children, adolescents, and adults with ADHD, sleep is a major issue. Around 25–50% of people with ADHD experience sleep issues and sleep disorders can be missed due to the similarity to other ADHD symptoms. Nightmares are very common for children with ADHD and this can be quite distressing, especially when it is recurring.

Doctors are beginning to realize the large number of sleep issues that go hand in hand with ADHD and there is a greater emphasis being placed on getting sleep issues treated. For you as a parent, I'm sure this is high up on your priority list. This is especially crucial since sleep issues tend to get worse as children go into the teenager stage.

One of the reasons children with ADHD struggle at bedtime is because their anxiety can spike. Anxiety is not just something we experience in our minds and so there is a real bodily reaction that gets in the way of being able to relax and settle for sleep. Imagine trying to sleep with a racing heart or sweating palms!

Some researchers believe that ADHD is linked with a delayed circadian rhythm and delayed melatonin production. If the internal body clock is off-kilter, then sleeping will be an issue, and waking up might be an even bigger one. Melatonin is a hormone that we make in our bodies and it's responsible for day cycles and sleep cycles. If a child has issues with melatonin and their circadian rhythm, it's going to be super important to support them in their sleep so they don't feel exhausted during the day.

Let's see how we can address sleep issues and increase the quality of sleep for our children.

1. **Cut out stimulants before bed.** This applies primarily to sugar and caffeine, although alcohol is also advised against (that will be more important as your child goes into adulthood, so save that tip for later!) If these stimulants can be avoided for the entire evening, even better again. It's not unusual that a person with ADHD would get a

sudden jolt of energy right before bed but it's good not to have anything that might be adding fuel to the fire.

2. **Checking Method.** This really involves the parent putting their child to bed, but checking in on them every few minutes. This might sound disruptive but it actually teaches your child that they are safe and that you are there. This helps to regulate their anxiety which will help them sleep.

3. **Camping in Method.** This is a really useful way of helping your child learn how to get to sleep. First, you as the parent would stay near your child, perhaps sitting by their bed as they settle in for the night. Slowly, at a pace that feels right for your child, you would start to move further away from them, until you are able to leave the room. You might need to try this for a while but it teaches your child that they are safe, and as you move away from them, they start to gain confidence in themselves too.

4. **Screen-Free Zones.** Try to get screen time all done and dusted at least an hour prior to bedtime. This applies to all screens!

5. **Bed = Stress-Free Zone.** So the bedroom is

screen and stress-free in an ideal ADHD world. This means no homework or projects are to be done in the bedroom. Bed is specifically for sleeping and this way, your child will be conditioning themselves to rest easier once they're in their bedroom.

6. **Get All the Energy Out.** For a child with ADHD, it's vital they get enough movement throughout the day. If their body is tired, they will be able to relax. If not, they might find it impossible to get to sleep at a reasonable time at all.

7. **Get Enough Sunshine.** This can be a tricky thing to do for a couple of reasons. If you live somewhere that doesn't get a lot of sunshine, then you might struggle here. If your child is in a lot of extracurricular activities and these take place indoors, this can be a difficult one to do. However, it's really great to know that sunshine can help a person with ADHD get better sleep. Sometimes we might not even know what will help so when we find out, it's a powerful tool in our kit.

8. **Same Bedtime and Wake Up Time.** This is a really important thing to build into a

child's routine as it will help train their internal body clock. They will begin to feel relaxed once it gets close to bedtime and they will begin to wake up easier in the mornings.

9. **Avoid Hyperfocusing in the Evenings.** If at all possible, it will be important to stay away from activities that require a high level of focus. This will help signal to your child's body clock that it's time to slow down and get to bed.

10. **Keep the Room Quiet and Dark.** The preparation of the environment will be so helpful in getting your child to sleep. Think about trying to sleep in a room that has too much noise, is the wrong temperature, or is too bright. It just doesn't help you get to sleep and when a person has ADHD, they can be distracted by the slightest detail. This distraction will keep them up and add to tiredness the next morning.

Sleep is a complex thing to master. There are factors at play that are out of our control, but there are many factors that are within our control. Things you cannot control are okay to think about from time to time, but try your very best to focus on things that you can amend and tweak.

There might be some factors that you've never considered and now you can focus your attention on adjusting them. Mastering bedtime and nighttime sleeping will be a positive result for both you and your child.

MANAGING ANGER

Amongst anxiety, sadness, and excitement, anger is an emotion that features heavily in the story of ADHD. Anger is a strong emotion and at times it can be volatile. Anger can also be a difficult emotion to witness and it can leave you feeling drained. It wouldn't be helpful to actively work against anger because it's a natural emotion that each person feels. And it's healthy to express anger.

That being said, your child might be prone to more angry outbursts than their peers. As they get older, you might be feeling more and more pressure to manage the anger so your child doesn't feel embarrassed by their outbursts. When a three-year-old throws a tantrum, there is no societal pressure to make it stop because everyone knows that tantrums are to be expected at that age. But when your child is 11 and they seem to be having a tantrum, we might find other people are less understanding.

So, anger is healthy and normal. But angry outbursts can be exhausting and there is no real need for as many. And unfortunately, anger can be an emotion that gets us into trouble. So, for us as parents, we need to slow down enough to help our children slow themselves down, even in an angry state.

> *Anger has been compared to a sneeze—it's necessary, but it should clear the passageway*
>
> — (HALLOWELL, 2022)

The anger shouldn't really be leftover and getting worse. And it's important to remember that a child who cannot express their anger or let it out at all, is not doing any better than a child who spills their anger everywhere. Both are in need of a change.

That's where you come in! You can help your child understand the triggers for their anger, the purpose of the emotion, as well as ways of neutralizing the strong emotion. It is helpful to know too what your relationship is to anger. If you need to take some time reflecting on your anger expression, be sure to give yourself the time and space to do so.

Let's take a look at ways of managing anger so it does not have a hold over your family:

- **Anger is a Signal, Not an Outcome.** Help your child slow down their anger by explaining (in age-appropriate terms) that it's vital to know why we're angry. Anger is not the end result and it's just showing us something isn't right for us. For example, your child might get angry during a game with friends. This might be a result of rule-breaking and it can be helpful for your child to understand that rules sometimes get broken. Additionally, you can help your child find the words to express that they like the rules being respected during games.
- **Emotion Thermometer.** Time to get your arts and crafts out here. When your child is feeling calm, ask them to draw a thermometer with five different levels. At the very bottom of the thermometer, ask them to write down words to describe

feeling calm. On the second level, they can write words to describe feeling excitement. On level three, they can start to write words that describe agitation. Make sure they use words that are comfortable and appropriate to them. It needs to be specific! On level four, so near the top, the child writes words to describe feeling angry, but not explosive. On level five, at the top of the thermometer, that's where they need to write words that describe feelings of rage. This thermometer can be decorated with corresponding colors, for example, blue for calm, black, or red for rage. This emotion thermometer will help your child figure out how to say where they're at, emotionally. You will be able to help your child verbalize their feelings and by doing so, this will bring down the anger.

- **Slave Punishment.** Do you remember Craig and Sam? While punishing a child at the moment might feel like the right thing to do, often it just makes the situation much worse. If you are feeling overwhelmed, and someone starts telling you why you're out of line, you aren't going to take their words in. The logical part of our brain does not listen when we are feeling an intense emotion. The only way to calm another person down is to meet their emotion, and then offer logic once the intensity has dropped. If your child is angry, try to acknowledge their anger before moving on to the consequences. If you can calm your child down, you've done your job as the parent. When your child is feeling calm, you can explain why their actions weren't really okay. Let your child know that you are not blindly out to punish them. Rather, you're trying to teach them about boundaries, consequences, and emotional intelligence.

- **Collaborate.** When your child is expressing anger, try to refrain from viewing the situation as a "You Versus Them" type of scenario. Try instead to work together and problem-solve. If your child is throwing items, instead of scolding them, stop them mid-throw and ask them what they need and what they want. If you can figure out what they're trying to achieve, you can problem-solve. There's no need to express disappointment, anger, or anything other than compassion in a heated moment. If you

can work with your child in the heat of the
moment, you'll be able to figure out a plan of
action for the next heated moment. If your
child feels like you are trying to work with
them, they will calm down easier.

- **Exercise Anger.** When we get enough
  exercise, our bodies and our brains work
  better. If you find that your child is having
  multiple angry episodes per day, something
  like physical exercise might help to regulate
  the energy that is building up in their
  system. If they aren't getting enough
  movement in their day, their agitation will
  only add fuel to the fire. This seems so
  simple to do but there are days when the
  weather, school, or other commitments
  might get in the way.

- **Figure out other Problems.** A child with
  ADHD is likely to have another issue and if
  this accompanying issue isn't understood or
  treated, then anger will seem like a more
  prevalent problem than it needs to be.
  Imagine having a problem that you can't
  communicate with, and other people cannot
  see. Every time you attempt to explain
  what's going on, people tell you that you

need to just calm down. Over time you would feel like you were going to burst with anger. For a lot of people, children and adults alike, it can feel infuriating living with conditions that other people do not understand. As the parent, try to keep notes on what you're seeing and really tune into what your child is saying and doing. This will help identify other issues that might be present. If your child had ADHD along with dyslexia, for instance, you might see a lot of anger around schoolwork. This might be down to the focus issues and the frustration around words and learning difficulty. It's up to us to see what is at play, and what we can do about it.

Most of the time, managing anger is about planning ahead and having a good relationship with your anger. If you are comfortable with anger, you won't feel terrified by tantrums, and nor will you feel affronted by them. If you can foresee the triggers in your child's say, you'll be able to prepare the environment so there is as little explosiveness as possible.

It's vital to understand that your child is more prone to anger, and that's okay. We all experience anger but we have different ways of letting it out. As long as your child knows that you are there to support them and help them to master their reactions, I think you will be ahead of the game.

REJECTION SENSITIVE DYSPHORIA

Rejection Sensitive Dysphoria (RDS) is an extreme emotional reaction to perceived criticism, rejection, or failure. The word *Dysphoria* comes from the Greek word *Dusphoria* which means "difficult to bear." When a person with ADHD experiences criticism, or even perceives criticism, it can feel painful. RDS goes with ADHD and it can cause major disruption in relationships because the person experiencing the emotional pain feels rejected, and the other person might feel shocked or hurt by the major emotional response.

In this case, the emotional reaction might be externalized and the person with ADHD might display a huge amount of rage. Sometimes, the feelings can be internalized, and the person might look as though they are experiencing a mood disorder such as depression, complete with suicidal ideation.

RDS can often be mistaken for mood disorders because on the outside it can seem as though the person was feeling completely fine, and now they are feeling low enough to speak about feeling worthless or suicidal. This might seem shocking but it's vital to understand that ADHD can cause a lot of distress in a person.

This is something that we need to really be aware of because otherwise, we could really be liable to just shake our heads and wonder why our child is taking things so personally, or getting so down when they believe they might have made a mistake. We spoke about how different a person's brain is when they have ADHD and this means they have trouble regulating their emotions, even when they have a huge desire to do so. RDS adds to this and it can be really difficult to navigate considering the emotional reaction that can happen, even when there wasn't any actual criticism or rejection.

It's important to remember that for the child with ADHD, the perception of it is just as real to them. They won't be calmed down just by another person trying to convince them that they're mistaken.

For an adult with RDS, they can become so fearful of experiencing criticism, that they might go out of their way to avoid any situation where they might experience it. For instance, they might avoid meetings with their boss, or they might skip situations where they will have to perform in front of others. This can look a lot like social anxiety but it's more accurate to say they want to avoid difficult situations where they will feel a lot of pain, if rejected or criticized.

You might be thinking of scenarios where your child wanted to skip school, or an extracurricular activity, and it's good to be aware of the circumstances surrounding these. For example, your child might love going to dance class, but as soon as there is a show, they might have headaches or a stomach ache, or high levels of anxiety. This can be a physical indicator that they are feeling extremely worried about what might happen.

So, how does RDS impact a person? There are certain adaptive behaviors that we might see and it's vital to know what these are so you can help your child in situations where they experience extreme emotional reactions.

Having an understanding is the first, and potentially most important, step.

1. **They Stop Trying.** A person with RSD might feel happy knowing that they can avoid something they love, as long as they also avoid criticism. This might be a trade-off that seems totally worth it. Feeling safe is *way* more important than taking part in activities that put us out there if we are terrified of criticism. Keep an eye out for this because it can be hard to miss. As children get older, they naturally change interests and hobbies. But if your child loves doing something, but won't ever do it anymore, RDS might be playing a part.

2. **People-Pleasing.** Your child might try absolutely anything to make everyone happy. They do this by paying close attention to the people around them and learning what makes them happy. Your child might start seeking a lot of praise and doing lots of things to earn that praise. It can take over their own needs and this can be a real tragedy. Imagine a person only living the way everyone else liked? We need

to help our children live the way they want to.

3. **Avoiding Social Situations.** So we've already touched on this one, but it's worth bearing in mind. Your child already struggles to focus and might interrupt a lot of the time. ADHD makes social situations more difficult and when you add RSD on top, your child might feel suffocated by their own worry. *What if this person makes fun of me? What if that person talks about the mistake I made earlier today? What will I do if they don't want to play my game?* It can feel like an overwhelming situation to get into and so avoiding might seem like the smarter option.

4. **Negative or Harsh Language.** You might see that your child speaks really harshly about themselves and others, and this can be a symptom of RDS. They might use words like 'stupid' to describe themselves and it can be difficult to intervene when they start speaking this way.

RDS is a part of emotional dysregulation that comes with ADHD and it can also contribute to low self-esteem, relationship issues such as feeling attacked, and rumination over uncomfortable or difficult situations. When you take all of this into consideration, it's not hard to see why some people appear to develop mood disorders. RDS can make everyday situations such as teasing feel painful and the explosive reaction can isolate the person with ADHD.

The only thing you can do to help your child with RDS is to support them in the situation and help them regulate their emotions as much as possible. When a person has RDS, the reaction is explosive and immediate, so there might be no warning signs ahead of them. Some adults with RDS take medication to help them but that is of course an individual decision for each person and family to make. Other than medication, it can be helpful to teach your child quick regulating exercises, especially ones that get their senses involved.

One simple exercise might include having a 'stress' ball or toy. Sensory toys are super helpful for a lot of children who are experiencing anxiety or stress, and if you can pick one out with your child, this can be something for them to hold and squeeze when they are getting overwhelmed. You know your child best and you know what will be most effective when it comes to sensory toys, but it's really great when your child can pick one out for themselves, and you make sure to carry it around wherever you go. It's not a miracle but it might slow down the emotional response.

If there are key tips to take away from this discussion, they are:

- Have patience with your child when they are feeling criticized or doing poorly in any activity.
- Help your child label their emotions so there's no added frustration in a heightened situation.
- Let your child's teacher know that criticism or failure might be a potential trigger and the successful ways you have found to calm your child down.

DYSLEXIA AND ADHD

When a child starts school, their ADHD is usually pretty obvious from the first days. A child with hyperactive ADHD will struggle to sit still, be quiet, or follow instructions. Teachers work with so many children that they can quickly see if a child has any differences in their attention or learning ability.

However, dyslexia is something that can be missed in the first few years of school. If a child has ADHD and dyslexia, dyslexia may be missed entirely.

For example, people with dyslexia have attention issues when it comes to reading demands. This could be mistaken for ADHD, even though the attention issues might not be present elsewhere for a person with dyslexia.

Dyslexia is often misunderstood. It's not about words being read backward or upside down as many people would have believed. For people with dyslexia, the processing of sounds and letters can be a challenge. Some people have problems with segmenting words which means they would read a word like 'doctor' as 'do–ctor' (Olivardia, 2020). Sometimes people with dyslexia have difficulties that occur in ADHD, namely information processing speed, working memory deficits, and naming speed (Olivardia, 2020).

The reason it's important to be aware of this is because if dyslexia were to go undiagnosed or unno-ticed, the symptoms could cause aggravation of existing ADHD symptoms. Like ADHD, dyslexia can cause a lot of self-esteem issues and this needs to be caught as early as possible so your child does not start to believe they are unintelligent if they struggle with reading.

Some of the similarities between dyslexia and ADHD are:

- Concentration issues in school, particularly during low stimulus tasks such as reading and writing. The inattention seen in ADHD will generally not be seen across the board for a person with dyslexia unless they also have ADHD.
- Self-esteem issues such as feelings of worthlessness. When a person has ADHD, they might feel as though they can never finish a task and this can lead to feeling stupid or incompetent. This is horrible to read as a parent, but it is an unfortunate piece of the puzzle sometimes. For a person with dyslexia, they might also feel 'slow' or unworthy if they are struggling with tasks that their peers seem to do okay with.

There are a few interventions that have been developed for dyslexia and this is wonderful news. These include specific reading interventions such as Orton–Gillingham (Olivardia, 2020). A lot of children who have both dyslexia and ADHD will do better with reading once their ADHD symptoms and triggers are managed. As a parent, you have a big job but it is worth your time and energy, as you already know.

How will I know my Child has Dyslexia and What Can I do?

As you can imagine, it might be really difficult to discern what behavior is down to ADHD, and what might be down to an issue such as dyslexia. If you are concerned about this, approach your child's teacher and health professionals. In my experience, you will have peace of mind if you know for sure what's going on. Your child will need to get assessed for dyslexia and this differs depending on where you're located. Your healthcare professional and teachers should be able to point you in the right direction.

Once your child has been formally diagnosed, you can seek reading interventions for him/her. These can be done in school and some teachers are wonderful at implementing specialized programs. Other ways that help include:

- Multi-Sensory Instruction in decoding skills (Martinelli, 2022).
- Intense intervention such as specialized reading programs.
- Teaching comprehension strategies so the child can understand what they are seeing.
- Drilling sight words.
- Decoding skills so a child can untangle the words for themselves.

Don't worry if you feel way out of your depth reading this. A lot of these strategies will be done by your child's teacher but that doesn't mean you can't learn how to help at home if you feel very strongly about it. The internet is a weird and wonderful place, and there are so many places you can connect with other people who can give you advice and tips. The main take-home point here is to reach out for help.

You can do it!

We've covered a lot of ground here! ADHD is so much more complex than it seems initially. You are doing the hard work by exploring what it means to have ADHD and anxiety, dyslexia, and RDS. ADHD is an intricate neurological condition and it presents itself in a multitude of ways. But don't give up hope, even on the bad days.

ADHD is a curveball you might not have expected, but it's something you can deal with and at the end of the day, your child is a wonder to behold. If we can slow down some of the emotions and the resulting explosions, we will be able to find time to slow down ourselves.

Some of the key points from this chapter are:

- Figuring out what conditions might be there, if any. For instance, if your child has ADHD and dyslexia, these will both need management to help your child feel supported and competent. Being aware that ADHD goes along with other issues such as dyslexia, is half the battle.
- Tailor bedtime for your child's needs. Whether

that includes camping or reducing screen time, there are actionable things you can do to help your child get a better night's sleep. Don't be afraid to do some research into melatonin or any other physical issues that might be at play.

- Anger is a healthy emotion and once you've addressed your relationship and perspective on it, you'll be better able to help your child address and cope with their anger.

- RDS is a reality for a lot of people living with ADHD. Be mindful of this, and don't be afraid to speak about it with your family and anyone else who may be important to your child's life.

- Anxiety, like anger, is a 'normal' feeling. However, if you feel that your child gets anxious an inordinate amount of the time, use some of the defusion techniques I've listed. These can really help control anxiety so it is not clouding your child's life.

This is a *huge* amount of information to take in and there is no shame in re-reading, and re-reading until you feel confident to get to work. In the next few chapters, we will also focus on how you can look after yourself because your child will prosper if you are feeling solid in yourself.

First, we will address how you can improve the quality of your child's life, and this is especially important if you are feeling weary in the ADHD journey. We're in this together, and you are doing your best.

Let's go!

5

SCHOOL = STRESS?

"All the good stuff is on the other side of tired."

— ANDRE AGASSI

You know the word 'weary' intimately. You have been best friends with 'tired' for a while now. How do I know this? Well, because this is universally true of any parent. Parenting is no joke. On top of that, having children with ADHD or neurodivergence adds an extra bonus level. Like I said earlier, I know you're doing a great job. It's good to acknowledge the difficulty every so often, too.

Most days will have lovely moments, with some hard moments sprinkled right in there.

We are going to address some key issues that crop up in discussions of ADHD. We are going to look at school refusal, which is when a child point blank refuses to go into school. This can be so frustrating and difficult to navigate, so it's well worth discussing. Another issue we will talk about is sibling problems and social exclusion. Unfortunately, there can be a lot of difficulties in these areas, and tools are needed to alleviate the stress that can be caused as a result.

These issues might be ahead of you on your parenting journey, or perhaps you've encountered these many times already. Let's stick with each other on this and don't feel like you need to implement every strategy, all at once. One step at a time is good enough.

80/20 FOR SUCCESS

First of all, we're going to talk about the Pareto Principle, otherwise known as the 80/20 rule. This is a key principle for ADHD and if you have never heard of it, this is your sign to try it out for yourself and your child.

In the late 19th century, Italian economist Vilfredo Pareto discovered that 80 percent of Italy's land was owned by 20 percent of the population. This was striking and Richard Koch wrote about this because it seemed to apply to a lot of things in life. Richard Koch wrote about how 80 percent of our desired outcomes were essentially a result of 20 percent of our efforts.

This is huge for many reasons and it looks as though it is particularly helpful for many people with ADHD. Why? Well, for a person with ADHD, they struggle to identify priorities. In a day, they might have 10 things to do, and each item looks the same in importance. They might feel like something is important because the person asking them for a favor is being quite persistent. If your child has multiple things to do in their day, they might do the most familiar thing even though it is time-consuming and slightly irrelevant to their day's goals.

A person with ADHD might see multiple options and get really overwhelmed by the choices. In that case, they would happily do an activity that is being asked of them persistently or is quite familiar to them. In some cases, they might feel like something is time-sensitive and they might choose to do that activity, even though it isn't what they need to do. The choices don't automatically sort themselves into a neat priority pile and the confusion can get over-whelming.

This is where the 80/20 rule comes in. Your child's success will be determined by 20 percent of their efforts. This means harnessing their ability to hyper-focus and using it for the most important things. For example, your child might struggle in the mornings getting ready for school. They might start looking for a school textbook, and you'll find them reorga-nizing their bookshelves, five minutes from go-time. If your child is able to focus for 20 percent of the morning, they will get most of their tasks done in that time.

So, how can we do this?

1. **Start with your goal.** Write down the goal and ignore the extraneous stuff. In the example above, the goal would be to get to school on time, with all of the necessary equipment. You could write down the

essential items, the leaving time, and the other details such as breakfast and outfit. This might only take two minutes to write down, and another two minutes to prepare for the morning. If everything is ready to go, your child will be ready much quicker and things won't get as distracting.

2. **Be as Specific as Possible.** If your goal is to get to school on time with everything necessary, then you need to be really specific. You would make sure that the coat your child needs is ready to go, the school books needed are in the school bag, and lunch is decided on and packed, if possible. For adults, this step might look like having car keys ready and having items like a phone charger if their phone battery tends to run out. Be specific and get into the details.

3. **Establish the Time Frame.** As I said, this might only take you a few minutes to write down, and a few minutes to complete. But you might want your child to come up with a reasonable time frame on their own, and they might decide that 15 minutes is more reasonable for them to complete the steps.

These 15 minutes will save the drama and extra time in the morning!

4. **Understand what the 80 percent of unnecessary tasks are.** So this would definitely include organizing a bookshelf. It might also include chores that can wait, fixing broken toys—you get the gist! With your child, figure out what does not need to get done right now.

5. **Compile all of the Info and Stick to it!** This sounds really easy, but it takes a game plan. Once you've identified the goal, the necessary steps, and what can be left aside, you need to put the plan into action.

This process can be repeated for each individual task and it might be a miracle time saver and frustration buster in your household. It sounds almost too good to be true that 20 percent of the effort is responsible for 80 percent of the outcomes, but this is something that you can try and if it works, embrace it. You might find that you could apply this to your task list or weekly to-dos. This is something that can really boost your child's self-esteem. Completing a task feels like a win and these little wins need to be celebrated.

The 80/20 rule can be applied to lots of areas and once you've gotten used to the principle, you might find that it can be applied to difficult areas. We're going to look at the topics I mentioned and we'll see where the 80/20 rule might slot in. For a lot of children with ADHD, we can apply the 80/20 rule to their symptoms. What I mean is that if we could manage 20 percent of the symptoms, 80 percent of the frustrations and difficulties could be managed.

This is super news and it's worth giving it a try!

ADHD AND SCHOOL

The struggle with school is intense. It's not for the faint of heart. I just want to start by saying this because there can be so much weariness or embarrassment around this topic. When a child refuses to go to school, this usually isn't a one-morning event. It can be an ongoing struggle and it's hard not to get overwhelmed or worn down as the parent.

For a lot of families, school is one of the biggest issues. School can be repetitive, boring, difficult, and tiring. Add ADHD to that mix and you now have a person who might be willing to learn, but unable to sit still or focus on what's being taught. If a child was desperately trying to do well, it would then be heart-breaking to constantly end up in trouble for their ADHD symptoms. Let's take an example.

Jake is a nine-year-old boy who likes going to school. He has lots of friends, his teacher has told him he's really funny, and he is pretty good at sports. He was diagnosed with ADHD when he was five, and his parents have done a lot of work at home, trying to support him with his symptoms. For the most part, Jake is doing really well and his ADHD doesn't seem to impact him negatively very often.

One morning, Jake gets into school and during assembly, a new adult is there. It turns out that Jake's teacher was called away on a family emergency and will be gone indefinitely. Jake isn't sure how he feels about this new person, and he's never had a male teacher before. The teacher is called Mr. Murphy, and he is relatively new to a career in teaching. At first things seem to be going okay in class, but Jake's mother notices that he is coming home in poor form. He has fights with some friends and there are emotional outbursts more frequently.

In the morning Jake has stomach aches and headaches. Soon Jake is trying to avoid school. When Jake's mother approaches the school and Jake's teacher, they are quite unhelpful. Jake's mother feels frustrated because the changes have only begun since Jake's teacher changed and she feels powerless to help her son. The school tells her that nothing has really changed and they say they will keep her informed of Jake's behavior.

Reading about Jake and his mother, what reactions came up for you? When dealing with external adults, it can feel difficult to get your point across. Unfortunately, schools are rarely equipped to have individualized plans for each child with the facilities and training to execute these plans. Aside from these kinds of facilities, it can be really difficult to communicate your child's needs to their teacher. Teachers are only human and they may or may not be open to adapting their teaching style.

This might seem shocking but it's good to be prepared for any kind of response. We'll look at onboarding your child's teacher and school because life will move more smoothly for your family when everyone is working together.

How to Onboard Your Child's School

In an ideal world, your teacher will understand your child and will have a good understanding of ADHD.

In some instances, a teacher will be able to help the parents get more information because they have encountered ADHD many times over. However, there are times when the teacher might be less helpful or even frustrated with a child's behavior.

In these cases, we need to work out how we can work with a teacher who is with our child every day of the school week. Onboarding is a term used to describe how people are integrated into a new environment and it's really about supporting someone in a new role so they can flourish.

For instance, if someone started a new job, onboarding would include familiarizing the new employee with the policies and work environment. Onboarding seeks collaboration and that's what we really need to do with our children's teachers. We can't assume that they know everything about ADHD and it is in everyone's best interest to work together.

- **Set up a Meeting.** As a parent of a child with ADHD, you will probably receive a few phone calls over the school year. If your child is struggling in school, you will need to make every effort to work with your child's school so effective problem-solving can happen. One way to make this process easier is to set up a meeting with your child's teacher and principal. A meeting in person will enable you to air out any of your concerns, and it will give them the opportunity to ask questions about your child's needs. By meeting in person, you will get a sense of how your school approaches ADHD and learning difficulties. This will put your mind at ease a little, and it will help you feel more confident in asking for more support.

- **Speak about the Hidden Elements of ADHD.** When we discussed the different kinds of ADHD and dyslexia, we talked about how some symptoms can be missed and some are written off as something else. It is really helpful for a teacher to understand the hidden elements of ADHD. For example, a teacher will easily see hyperactivity but they might miss out on the feelings of worthlessness or the sensitivity to failure. It can be so helpful for your child's teacher to be made fully aware of what triggers your child's emotional outbursts.

The teacher might also be able to shed light on how your child operates in the classroom so you can really work as a team. Some hidden elements you might want to discuss are sleep disturbance, impaired sense of time, and feelings of inadequacy.

- **Talk Specifics on Health.** If your child is taking any medications, your child's teacher needs to know. The details they ought to know are the side effects and the symptoms they are aiming to treat. This is crucial because for the hours your child is in school, the teacher will be able to tell you if the symptoms are present. If your child has any sensory issues or any other issues such as anxiety, it is imperative that their teacher knows. More information usually means more support. If an adult believed a child's behavior was purposeful and voluntary, they might understandably react with frustration or discipline. If an adult is aware of a child's neurodivergence, they will be much more aware of what that means for learning.

- **Strategize Together.** Let your child's teacher know what works and what definitely doesn't work for your child. They might have some great ideas too, so make use of the pooled knowledge and coordinate. There will be new techniques that educators might be aware of that parents aren't, and vice versa.

- **Be Open.** Don't feel like you have to know everything about ADHD just because your child has it. You are the expert on your child, not on every child with ADHD. Let the teacher tell you things that you may not have known and don't judge yourself for not having the answers sometimes.

School Going Refusal

It is really common for children to refuse to go to school from time to time. If you can reflect on your childhood, there were probably a ton of times when you didn't want to go either. School isn't always fun and it's natural to want breaks, even when you've just had a holiday from school. But when a child is seriously rejecting school and fighting with their parents every morning, it becomes really exhausting and distressing for everyone involved. Each child is individual but there are certain elements of school refusal that are common.

For example, a lot of children will say they feel unwell every morning. They might have headaches, stomachaches, vomiting, or an inability to eat. They might cry or throw tantrums and this can be really upsetting. As a parent, you don't want to send your child to school if they are sick but if you're noticing a pattern, it can be hard to stay patient.

It can be difficult to know exactly why your child isn't going to school, or what is triggering the refusal. In most cases, a child might avoid school because of the emotions it triggers within them. For example, if there is anxiety about going to school, the child will seek the comfort and security of being at home. At home, we have all of the items we need and are used to. We know what to expect from our home environment.

At home, we have our safe base with mom and dad, or whoever we spend the most time with. The secure feeling at home can make schools feel even less secure when there are issues arising. For example, if home is really calm and comforting, a school culture with pervasive bullying will feel even worse. It is good to note that if there are issues at home, school refusal might still happen.

If life feels quite unsteady, a child might try to shield themselves from awkward situations outside of the home even more. It might be that a child can handle the uncertain environment of home, but not the uncertainty of school. In either situation, a child might be trying their best to gain control of what's happening around them.

If a child has learning difficulties, school will be a minefield. It might be okay academically, but socially it can be difficult. Or the social side might be absolutely fine, but the classroom engagement feels too hard. My main point here is that school is a complex experience in the best circumstances. If a child is working with ADHD or other issues like dyslexia, then school will be even more advanced and complicated.

When we sit with this information and then consider social factors, bullying, puberty, and all of the other experiences of childhood and adolescence, it's not too surprising that some kids would rather stay at home at any cost.

Has your child ever refused to go to school, or social activity? If so, what do you feel was underlying the refusal? Perhaps you've dealt with this issue successfully, or perhaps you've never experienced school refusal. No matter where you're at, this is a common issue that we need to be able to address when it comes up.

Some practical ways you can help your child overcome their anxiety around going to school are:

- **Believe in Them.** Let your child know that even though they might have missed school, you know they can build up their confidence and get back into school. If you give up hope, your child will sense this on some level so it's important to remain calm and look at the bigger picture. If your child misses a few weeks of school over their entire school years, this won't be the end of the world. Let them know that everything is going to be okay.
- **Maintain Good Contact.** Even though you might be tired or frustrated, remain in contact with your child's teacher and school. Feeling like you have other people who understand the situation will help you feel like you can get your child through this period.
- **Let Your Child Take in a Token.** Some items of yours might help your child feel less

anxious when they are away from you. You might give them a small picture of you, or maybe a little token such as a keyring. Some parents find it helpful to give their child a spare key because the child knows that mom or dad has to come back to get the key, if nothing else. You can ask your child what item they'd like to take with them and see what works.

- **Let Your Child Name Their Fears.** Sometimes a child will feel at ease once you let them air out the thoughts that come to their mind ahead of school. Whatever we fear can feel so enormous until someone else lets us say it out loud, and allows us to name exactly what the fear is. Try not to judge the fear or laugh it off, because the fear is very real for your child. If you can trust yourself to hear them out, your child will be more likely to trust you and come to you when things feel too big.

- **Practice Separating.** No child likes being left without their parents, especially in the earlier years. Instead of not doing it because they don't like it, try to build up the positive experiences. You could try leaving them for

15 minutes with a family member a couple of times a week, and then start building up the time frame until they eventually get used to you going away, and coming back. This might seem irrelevant for school but it's honestly so important for your children to know that when you leave, you come back. It's really vital for children to learn that they will be okay, even if mom or dad is gone for a while. And as parents, we need to remember that it's our job to help our children build up a skill in this area and a tolerance for separation. Babies don't naturally know how to separate so we shouldn't be so hard on our children when they find separation really painful.

- **Be on Time.** So this is really important when a child has issues around school refusal. The anxiety your child has endured throughout the day will only increase if you intermittently show up late for pick-up time. Being on time is natural for a lot of people, but for some of us, it comes with practice. It needs a lot of preparation if you have a busy schedule, but showing up on time sends the signal to your child that you are there for them and you will make sure they are safe. It is really reassuring. If you are going to be late, or if another person is picking your child up, try to communicate this in advance to your child. If they know what's happening, children will be a lot calmer.

There are lots of strategies that you might find work well, and there might be some strategies that your child's teacher knows are helpful for your child. Keeping a close eye on the situation at home and school, and being hopeful that things will get better, will help you approach school refusal in a way that hopefully minimizes the amount of school time lost.

By staying in contact with the teacher, you can keep each other up to date on how things are going. Your teacher will be able to help your child find places that are 'safe' and can organize calming environments for high anxiety situations such as tests. In an ideal situation, all the adults are on the same team and working in a unified manner.

Dealing with Bullying

Bullying is an unfortunate experience for lots of people. Children with ADHD may feel like they have brought bullying upon themselves by their behavior and it's the parents' job to reassure them that this is never, ever true. Bullying is never the fault of anyone, except the bully. Let's just get that out of the way first of all!

A lot of kids with ADHD have an "out of sight, out of mind" way of thinking and so they might not tell you about social issues at school unless you directly ask them (Richfield, 2022). As a parent, it's good to ask your child about their friends, who they play with, and what the other kids are like at school. Very quickly you'll notice if there seem to be any red flags.

Things your child might say that you might need to keep an eye out for include:

- Saying no one plays with them at break time.
- Repeating negative or teasing comments that another child has said.
- Saying mean things about themselves that they've been told by another person.
- Losing more things than usual at school, or coming home with their belongings broken.

There might be other things that alert you to any bullying going on. If your child is being bullied or has been in the past, try to acknowledge that it's not your fault. There can be a lot of guilt that sits with a parent after a bullying situation but it's never the fault of the child, or the parent. Bullies bully because of their own issues. It's heartbreaking to learn about bullying but there are things that can be done to make sure your child does not lose all self-esteem.

If your child is being bullied, try to explain how bullies work. Try to let them know that bullies choose whoever they think is an easy person to pick on. By no means is it ever a child with ADHD's fault, but as a parent, it can be good to let them know which of their behaviors people might find easy to bully. Speaking out at inopportune times, moving around a lot, or making a lot of jokes might all be things that draw unwanted attention.

These can be things your child is unaware of doing and it's important to speak to your child in a way that does not ever communicate that they are the problem. The bully is the problem. Your child might find that "low profile behavior" is helpful in staying away from bullies and this behavior includes using a quieter voice, watching out for listening, looking out for social cues, and keeping comments brief (Richfield, 2022).

If there is bullying happening, let your child's school know. Schools have a responsibility to ensure each student's well-being and bullying can have serious implications if it isn't dealt with well. Don't be afraid to approach the school to speak with them. Let them know what's been said, and ask them for help with the situation. If the bullying has happened, you need to nip it in the bud.

This is something that could impact your child's self-esteem and it can be a contributing factor to school refusal in a lot of cases. If your child's teacher sees some of the bullying happen, they will be able to intervene. Building up your child's self-confidence if they've been bullied will be important to keep in mind.

Helping with Schoolwork

Children with ADHD have obstacles that get in the way of school. These obstacles are troublesome across their lifetime, but school is where the difficulties are brought into sharp contrast. If a child has great strategies in place, they can do really well in school and they can grow their confidence. If there are no real helpful strategies in place, the child might feel stupid and hopeless towards school. Losing homework and forgetting what assignments are due are all too common experiences in ADHD.

Ask your child to sit at the front of the class. This might sound like a punishment, but it's a really effective way of reducing distractions in the classroom. By sitting near the front, your child will be able to look at their teacher for most of the lesson, and not get distracted by what's going on around them. The harder it is for them to slip through the cracks, the better. This means that if they start joking around or passing notes, the teacher will be able to notice right away. This will reduce the amount of time the child ends up distracted and it helps keep them accountable.

Organize playdates. A child with ADHD might find it really difficult to maintain friendships and this can be anxiety-inducing for both you and your child. If you organize playdates for your child, you can let them know what is expected of them. Knowing what comes next, and what they need to do, will help alleviate any social anxiety that might be present for your child. It will also help maintain friendships until your child can manage this alone.

Calendars are your friend. Time management is the eternal battle in ADHD. If you can help your child manage their time effectively, you will be helping them to manage the majority of their problems (Remember that 80/20 rule?) You can put a calendar up in your kitchen to help remind your child when there is a test or other event coming up. You can get your child a timer to help them transition between tasks. Timers are really helpful in addition to calendars, and anything that helps your child get their tasks done on time will help them feel confident and competent. Getting things done on time also helps reduce stress and feelings of worthlessness.

Find a concentration aid. Each person is different and some noises work better for your child than others. For example, your child might find a white noise machine really helpful, or maybe they find it too distracting. Did you know about pink noise or brown noise? You can also try water sounds. There is an abundance of focus tools and it's exciting when you find one that works really well.

Exercise. It seems like generic advice to say "eat well, move more" but in the case of ADHD, this is also hugely important for focus. If your child has had a long day of sitting, they will need after-school activities that get them moving. This can be scheduled for right after school so your child can focus on homework when they get home. Trying to get your child to shift between one sitting activity to another will rarely go well and these movement breaks will increase the chance of the homework actually getting done. Exercising regularly will also help your child regulate their emotions and so the explosiveness that comes with dysregulation should reduce, too.

Practice communicating educational needs. As the parent, you will be speaking with every teacher your child has. Speak to your child about their educational needs, and let them know a few pointers that you've learned along the way. Help your child speak for themselves so they become more confident, and learn that people will listen to them when they speak. They might only need to explain one or two elements of their ADHD experience but this will help them get more involved in their own needs and experience.

Practice beginning again. If all else fails, start from the start. For kids who have 'failed' socially, academically, or otherwise, starting again is a chance to let go of the past. Let your child know that tomorrow is always a new day, and there is no need to put pressure on ourselves to get something right quickly. If you can encourage your child to try again after things haven't gone well, then you will be teaching resilience. That's something we could all use more of!

There are many ways you can help your child progress well in school, a lot of things will only come with time. Be patient with yourself! Be patient with your child. Things will turn out okay, but it's a hard slog getting there.

Homeschooling

Have you ever wondered what life would be like if your child was homeschooled? In some parts of the world, this is pretty common. In others, it would be a really radical decision. Either way, it's worth understanding!

Homeschooling is an option that is often not explored enough. If you don't know anyone who homeschools, you might feel too overwhelmed to do most of the research needed to make an informed decision. If your child goes to traditional schools and manages okay, then homeschooling doesn't need to be explored. But, that's not the experience a lot of kids have. Children with ADHD are sometimes let down by their school, and the experience leaves a bad taste in everyone's mouth.

Children with ADHD might be left behind in school, bullied, misunderstood, and in a position where they are feeling like a failure. In these circumstances, parents want to find an option that will help build up their child's confidence once more. Home-schooling can sometimes be that option.

Homeschooling is not about replicating the school environment at the kitchen table. If that were the case, it would be of no benefit to making the switch from traditional schooling to homeschooling. There are many styles of homeschooling and the experience can be tailored to your child's learning needs. You could choose to homeschool through methods such as Montessori, Classical, or Char-lotte Mason, to name a few. These all have various benefits and drawbacks, and as a parent, you can ascertain which suits your child and their personality.

The overall benefits of homeschooling include:

- Being aware of what your child is learning and where they need to improve.
- Removing additional stressors specific to

ADHD, such as lateness, forgetting school materials, and detention.

- Having more freedom for movement breaks and creative activities.
- Being able to move at your child's pace so they can move quickly through tasks they find easy and have more focused time on difficult subjects.
- Being able to tailor the curriculum to your child's needs.

Homeschooling requires a time commitment from the parent and some parents find it easier to change their work to accommodate a homeschooling environment. Whatever style you choose for homeschooling, it needs to suit the child. There are so many styles to choose from that you are sure to find something that suits your child. What's more, homeschooling allows the child to learn in whatever ways suit them, whether that's auditory, visual, kinesthetic, or tactile. It's an approach to learning that really places the child at the center.

Homeschooling can be a fantastic experience, but it can also be less than ideal for some families. As you might imagine, there are some disadvantages to homeschooling. These disadvantages are significant considerations and the decision to begin home-schooling cannot be made lightly.

To homeschool, you will need both the time and energy to support your child to study. You will need to have a space in your home for schooling and for a lot of subjects you will need access to the Internet and a home computer. Your child will need additional hobbies so they can interact with other children their age because it could turn into an isolating experience if your child is not involved in social activities outside of the home.

As your child gets older, they might have negative feelings about being homeschooled. They might feel as though they missed out on a lot of experiences, especially if they started homeschooling from a very young age. You might feel frustrated with this but it's understandable for a young person to feel like the grass is greener on the other side. Ultimately, you need to make the decision on your child's education and once you've considered all options, the outcome will be okay.

THE STORY SO FAR

After looking at the various elements of school and ADHD, what does your gut tell you? Do you feel like great communication with your child's teacher is the key for your family? Does homeschooling sound like a dream or a nightmare? When you read through the practical tips for helping your child deal with schoolwork, was there anything that seemed like a 'eureka!' moment? If school refusal is a major issue in your household, do you feel a little more confident in approaching it?

This is your space to reflect and just think about how school impacts your child, yourself, and your family.

The take-home messages from this portion of our journey are:

- Don't give up! There are many methods of approaching school issues and not everyone will work for your child. Your main job is to keep trying.
- Communicate with your child's teacher. This might be the amazing collaboration that your child needs.

- If you can manage 20 percent of your child's ADHD symptoms, for example, time management and emotional regulation, you will see results in around 80 percent of their day.
- Bullying, social issues, and academic failure are all hardships your child might face. Your role as a parent is to equip them as best you can to face these challenges and to stay strong in yourself so your child has a solid foundation in the home.

School is a huge part of each child's life. By focusing on what you can do to improve it, you are setting the path to success and happiness for your children, trust me! In the next chapters, we will be looking at ADHD in adolescence, as well as sibling and neighbor issues. As your child gets older, it will be vital to have an insight into what you can do so they thrive outside the home.

6

ADHD AND YOUR TEEN

"Motherhood: the days are long, but the years are short."

— GRETCHEN RUBIN

When you first become a parent, the idea of one day having an adult child is preposterous. It's laughable! But then, days turn into weeks, months, and years. Suddenly you don't have a baby or a toddler anymore, and your child is starting to gain independence.

When your children get older, life changes in beautiful and surprising ways. All of a sudden you don't need to hold their hand crossing the road and they're able to cook some of the meals. There are lots of ways life changes and it's a joy to witness.

When your child with ADHD gets older, their symptoms manifest a little differently. They might not run around so much but the hyperactivity will still be visible to you as their parents. A huge part of our job as parents is to prepare our children for life outside the home. As they get older, they'll spend less and less time at home. It's imperative they have skills to make life fun and manageable.

We are going to take a look at ADHD outside the home as well as how it can impact sibling relationships. I have two children with ADHD diagnoses, but I also have one without it. ADHD runs in families but it's interesting to see how it influences family dynamics and situations.

SIBLINGS

Understanding the various challenges ADHD presents, it would be reasonable to assume that there are fights on an hourly basis between siblings. If there's more than one child in a house, there's bound to be arguments. But when one child has ADHD and a sibling without it, there seems to be less fighting happening. This is surprising information considering how stressful some situations can be with ADHD. Siblings of children with ADHD grow up accepting the symptoms and understanding the triggers for their brother or sister.

This is lovely because they accept their brother or sister for who they are. In another sense, this might be problematic because they might be too accepting of bad behavior. They might feel like emotional explosions are a fact of life and there's nothing to be done about them.

It's a delicate balance parenting children who are so different from one another and there are a few key things the parent needs to keep in mind so their typically developing child does not get overshadowed by ADHD.

Remaining Consistent and Fair. When a child with ADHD starts shouting or throwing things, it's important for their parents to discipline them effectively. We don't want to punish the child for having emotions, but we also don't want to let things slide when we wouldn't for a typically developing child. Things need to be fair for children because they have such a strong sense of right and wrong. If one child is allowed to do something 'naughty,' then their sibling will build up resentment when they are punished for the same behavior. It's the parent's role to keep the playing field even and fair.

Involving Siblings. When there's ADHD in the family, the siblings will be understanding of the symptoms without very much explanation. Having said that, it's good to be clear with everyone in the family about ADHD and all that it entails. Adhd is nothing to be afraid of or ashamed of, and it will be good to have open communication about it with the child diagnosed and the children who are typically developing. Involving the siblings might lift a load off everyone too. For example, if Sarah knows that her little brother James has trouble in the mornings, she could redirect him to his visual schedule or she could help him find his timer.

Sarah's job isn't to do everything for James but it's alright for her to step in when she notices a few little things are building up and adding to the chaos. If Sarah woke up feeling grumpy or tired, there would be no obligation on her to do the same the next morning. It's good enough that she's aware of his struggles and she can help him if need be. After all, Sarah is just a kid and she shouldn't have to worry about how James is going to get on. That load is for the parent to shoulder.

Tuning in to silence. If you have multiple children, do you feel like each one is heard equally? This is a tough question to ask yourself and it's not meant as a way to beat yourself up. You are trying your best and if ADHD takes over some days, that's okay. You might feel like you're putting out fires and in the midst, other things can be missed. That's just life. But if you feel like your typically developing child is not being heard, then it's time to become aware of where that's happening. If a child is keeping their struggles to themselves, then they might be shouldering a heavy load alone. Some children don't want to worry mom or dad and this is too much responsibility for a person so young. This is not what any parent wants for a child. We need to notice the silences in our children and we need to make sure that each child is getting what they need.

What about sibling rivalries? Well, with ADHD there will also be the rivalries and disagreements seen in every family. That's normal and to be expected. I believe it's really important to keep an eye out for how ADHD is impacting the family and any siblings. If children feel like any of their brothers or sisters are getting special treatment, this can add resentment over time.

In an ideal situation, children would completely support each other and accept each other. If you can work towards this in your home then you will be doing an amazing job as a parent.

Raising a child while you have ADHD

Being an adult with ADHD adds a new layer of complexity to parenting. The issues and symptoms that were present in childhood might be more manageable, but they do not go away entirely. A child with ADHD develops into a teen with ADHD, who then becomes an adult with...you guessed it, ADHD! So what happens when that adult has a child of their own with ADHD?

There are a few issues that might come up, but there's no real need to panic. ADHD tends to run in families and when symptoms aren't understood or managed, there can understandably be a lot of stress.

Here are some ways you can make sure both you and your child are not lost in a haze of confusion, frustration, and disorganization:

- Create visual cues and leave them around the house.
- Consistent mealtimes and bedtimes. As much as possible, have a consistent structure and routine for the entire family.
- Be creative. Both you and your child will benefit from some creativity. Leave sticky notes on the fridge, or set a funny name on your alarm. Anything that adds a bit of fun into your day, while also helping with organization.
- Organize your space the way you like. If you have the resources to invest in some new kitchen organizers, go for it. Dinner time will be streamlined if things are easier to find.
- Adjust your expectations of yourself and your child. Allow room for error and don't be too hard on yourself or your child.
- Give one instruction at a time.
- Get outside help where possible. If you need to bring in a babysitter once a week so you can catch up on housework, then don't feel bad about that. Not everyone can afford a housecleaner or childminder but if you can, and you feel you need it, go for it.

These are simple ways of alleviating some of the stress ADHD adds to a household. If you are an adult with ADHD, then I'm sure you have plenty of things you would add to that list. Try these tips out for size and see if they can help.

SLEEPOVERS

As your little person gets older, they will be out and about a lot more often. You might feel excited about this and there might be a real sense of achievement. You got them to that place in their lives and you've done a brilliant job, even if it doesn't feel like it some days. So when your child goes out for excursions like a school trip or a sleepover, you can pat yourself on the back that you've raised a confident child.

However, sleepovers and school overnight trips can be anxiety-provoking for the child and maybe even more so for the parent! It's really difficult to know when your child is ready but there are a few things that might help with the preparation.

Family practice. Has your child ever gone for sleepovers with cousins or their grandparents? If your child has never stayed away from you then it would be a good idea to try a night away from home with a family member. Some children are super confident when they spend the night away from home, but some kids take a little longer to settle into it. Any adult that can help you practice overnights needs to be drafted in to help!

Say goodbye to pressure. There's no specific age that is exactly right for a sleepover or night away from school. If you believe your child is ready at nine, then that's great. If you don't feel like your 10-year-old is confident enough just yet, then accept that and let go of any external pressure. Every child is different and there's no rush.

Notice maturity levels. Some children with ADHD will be less mature than their peers and will miss social cues, especially when they are dysregulated. Your child might not be ready for nights away from their family until they are into adolescence, and that's okay. If you're worried about your child getting really worked up while they're away, try to let the adults in charge know that you're okay with picking your child up any time of the night.

Make a game plan. So, your child is heading to a friend's house. Let the other parent know how to soothe your child if they get upset, and also what necessitates a phone call. For example, you might want to be contacted if your child has a minor injury or needs any pain relief. You might want to be called if they vomit, or if they are fighting with another child. ADHD can make social situations very difficult and a sleepover is a complex social engagement. There might be some anxiety or separation issues going on too, so it's best to have a good game plan. You could tell your child that you are going to collect them, no matter what.

By communicating your availability, you will reassure them that everything is going to be okay. You could leave written instructions on dietary requirements and other important information. If your child is taking medication, you will need to leave written instructions. We can't assume that a child can communicate their needs effectively when they are young so it's best just to have it all laid out for the adult in charge.

Host a sleepover. A great way of alleviating any anxiety your child might be feeling about a sleepover is to host a sleepover yourself. Sometimes children do much better when they are the host. For a person with ADHD, it can be much more relaxing to have other people come over. If anything goes wrong, the child with ADHD has the person who calms them down right there. If your child starts having an explosion, they might calm down a lot better in their own environment. Like having a night over with grandma and grandpa, this is a great way to warm your child up for nights away from their home.

Sleepovers are a big milestone and not every child loves them. That's okay! But for a lot of children, this is a great part of growing up. It's best to start small and if possible, to start sleepovers with adults your child is comfortable with. If they are comfortable with sleepovers, they'll do much better on school trips too. If your child is comfortable with their teacher, they'll feel much more confident and brave setting out on their school excursions.

As you can see, the factors that guarantee success during sleepovers will also be the factors that make school trips a success.

When Neighbors and Adults Struggle with Your Child's Behavior

Not every person is understanding. That's a hard truth and I'm sure you already know this but it's worth saying nonetheless. Even the most under-standing adult will have occasions where they feel less than patient. We need to be realistic in our expectations of other people so we don't take nega-tivity personally. I don't know about you, but almost everything feels personal when it's related to my children!

Your neighbors and friends will inevitably ask about your child and how they are getting on in school, friendship-wise, etc. It's true that a lot of children with ADHD will be evidently a little different from their peers. In one way it's lovely that other adults will speak to you about your child and there can be comfort found in those conversations.

In another sense, it can be a difficult position to be in too. Some adults won't be understanding and there might be some rude comments along the way. On explosive days you might feel like you need a shoulder to cry on, and the adults that make you feel heard are the ones you'll need to reach out to.

Whether you live in a neighborhood or out in the countryside, you will have some neighbors. These people could be negatively impacted by a child with ADHD (although, this is unlikely for the most part, don't worry!)

Maybe your child makes impulsive decisions and winds up throwing rocks at passing cars. Or maybe your child breaks a lot of rules during games and upsets the other children on the street. There are a myriad of ways that wires can be crossed and it's crucial you feel able to deal with the fallout.

Speak to your neighbors about any issues you've been dealing with regarding ADHD. You don't have to go into much detail at all, but some understanding will mean your neighbors will get why your son is behaving the way he is. Similar to onboarding your child's teacher, your neighbor will feel better able to approach you if anything happens. Opening up a dialogue with your neighbor enables clear communication and there is less opportunity for wires to get crossed.

Teach your child how to apologize when they've hurt another person or violated a boundary. This is huge and it can go a long way in creating and maintaining good neighborly relations. If your child throws rocks at a neighbor's car, explain why that's not okay, and bring your child to the neighbor to acknowledge what they did and apologize. This will show your child that respect is important and that when we make mistakes, we can say something to try and make it better.

Ask your neighbors about their children. When we have a child who is experiencing some delay or difficulty, it can be hard to remember that other children have difficulties too. Remember to ask other people how they are doing, and how their children are doing. This is not really just an onboarding issue, it's more of a good communication issue. This is a gentle reminder that sometimes the child with ADHD is doing pretty okay when it comes right down to it.

For the most part, being open to clear communication will prevent a lot of issues from developing. When we feel too afraid to speak up or ask for help, we let things add up which does nobody any favors.

SOCIAL EXCLUSION

Similar to bullying, social exclusion is a difficult topic when considering our children. No one wants their child to experience rejection in social situations. Seeing our children hurt and upset can make us feel helpless. But social rejection and exclusion are something we need to address and be aware of because it happens much more often for those living with ADHD. Some studies have found that 13 percent of young children experience social rejection in a classroom setting.

When we look at ADHD, that number rises to almost 60 percent. So that would mean that three out of five children with ADHD experience some form of exclusion. I know that hurts to hear and it's really not what we want to believe happens.

Why does ADHD contribute to social exclusion? For a lot of children, their symptoms of hyperactivity, inattention, and misreading of social cues mean that their peers develop a dislike within minutes of the meeting. A child with ADHD might fight more easily and they will have impulsivity during games and class time. Children will notice when one of their peers is talking over everyone and causing disruption. Unfortunately, this causes exclusion, and the child with ADHD doesn't necessarily have the social skills to address the issue or speak to a teacher about what's happening.

Your job as a parent is to help your child learn the social skills and emotional regulation necessary to make social connections with peers. Your role is to guide your child through the minefield of games, social events, and school. I say minefield because although we take these experiences for granted, they are horrendously difficult to navigate when you are doing these with ADHD.

One way of helping your child avoid social exclusion is to help them build up their social skills. You can do this by facilitating playdates, especially when your child is young. A playdate is such a simple way to observe how your child is interacting with other children. You will see how they deal with losing and rule-breaking. You'll notice any changes in their mood and you'll be able to step in if there's a serious fight about to happen. Let's take an example.

Georgiana has a four-year-old son called Aaron. Aaron has ADHD and really struggles with kids his age. He often plays by himself and does not play games with groups. Georgiana feels worried about Aaron and is trying to help him interact with his peers a little better. She organizes a playdate with her cousin Loretta and her daughter Sharon. Sharon is five and she has a bubbly character. Georgiana explains to Aaron that a family member is coming over to play for the afternoon.

Aaron doesn't seem overly pleased about having to share his toys and space, but once Sharon comes with her mother, he quickly shows her his favorite cars and rockets. Sharon is a little older and her emotional and social knowledge allows her to be patient with Aaron when he gets angry. She is patient but she also reminds him of the rules whenever she needs to.

Georgiana feels her anxiety slip away a little. Aaron does not lash out or hit and when Sharon is leaving, she gives him a hug. Aaron tells her everything he wants to do the next day they play and Georgiana can see that Aaron has some ability to play with other children. She also accepts that maybe he needs a lot more one-to-one playdates and these will help him interact in groups, later on.

By hosting playdates, you will allow your child to practice their skills in a space where they feel safe. They might feel apprehensive about sharing but any situation, like a sleepover or playdate allows you the opportunity to explain to your child what is expected of them. Your child needs practice, practice, practice when they are living with ADHD.

Social cues will not be obvious for children with ADHD but the great thing is that these can be learned over time.

When social exclusion is happening, you need to be able to encourage your child to try again. Not necessarily with the children excluding your child, but with their peers. It's important to gain resilience and to see that not every interaction will be negative. You might need to host playdates as Georgiana did, and with many different children. By exposing your child to different people and different situations, you are gearing them up for the social world.

Part of resilience is assisting your child in seeing the world as it is. Not everyone will like us, and that's okay. You could speak to your child about connection and friendships, and highlight the fact that there are people out there for all of us. Some people will be mean, and that's nothing to do with anyone other than them. You might ask your child if they like every person they've ever met. If he or she is being honest, the answer will be 'no!' It's okay to like some people more than others, although it's not polite to say it out loud.

Your child might encounter social setbacks but the main thing to watch out for is their self-esteem. If your child is rejected socially but still believes they are a cool person, then hallelujah! That's great. A kid who is managing life with ADHD is dealing with barriers others will never see. If they can make it through the early years and still believe in themselves, then you can celebrate your success as a great role model and supporter.

DE-ESCALATION TECHNIQUES

We've looked at explosiveness and what to do when it occurs—e-escalating a child that is overwhelmed is no easy task. The techniques that help us as parents are good to spread around so other adults know how to help if they're left in charge of your child at any point.

De-escalating a situation essentially means calming it down before it gets any worse. If a child is having a huge reaction to something that's happened, then there are a few key things that need to happen.

- Empathizing with the child will help them get their words out, and allow them space to communicate what's going on.
- Non-judgmental listening is so important in these situations because the emotions are

overwhelming for the child, and judgment will only add fuel to the fire.

- Bringing the child to a quiet space, or moving away from the fight. A tiny bit of distance will allow the child to cool down a bit, without lots of attention.
- Avoid overreacting. This will only add a level of anger or guilt.
- If you have to give in, give in early before things get to a level 10. In other words, pick your battles and do what you can to calm the situation before it gets too extreme. Once things have calmed down, then you can explain what the consequences or discipline might be.
- Stay calm and label the emotions you are noticing. For instance, you can say "I see you're pretty angry right now."

If you are coming from a judgmental space, you'll find that heightened situations will only reach new heights. When you can see the situation from the child's point of view, you are more likely to be able to help them calm down.

Parenting is difficult no matter what hand you are dealt. But when we approach it thoughtfully and practically, we will find that most issues can be resolved.

One thing we haven't touched on much is medication and self-care. We'll take a look at these and see what changes could be incorporated into everyday life.

7

MEDICATION PROS AND CONS

"I had to start being aware of what I ate, what I'm planning to eat, and take my twice-daily medication accordingly. That's not so difficult now, but when you're 10 years old, it's tough, let me tell you."

— DANA HILL

edication is a tricky conversation topic. It's a polarizing choice for conversation, and never more so than when it involves children. I'm not a health professional and I'm not trying to convince you of its inherent good or badness. As a parent, I like to have all the information available to me and I'd like to put that forward for you, too.

Let's take a look at medication for ADHD and what it offers. Like any medication, there are pros and cons and it's up to us to have some awareness of what these are.

WHERE DID THE MEDICATION START?

You might be as surprised as I am to learn that an early medication was found to help children with hyperactivity, as far back as 1937. The medication was Benzedrine and a medical Director called Charles Bradley found that it helped some children perform better in school, while also improving their behavior. It was approved in 1936 but it took a long time before researchers verified Bradley's discovery.

ADHD wasn't known by the same terminology as today, but it was discussed as far back as 1902. There were lectures given by Sir George Frederic Still on how some children with high intelligence seemed to struggle with impulsivity and hyperactivity. It's amazing to know that ADHD is not a 'new' occurrence and we've just gotten better at finding it and treating it.

In the 1940s, Ritalin was marketed for children with ADHD. Today it's more commonly known as methylphenidate. It was launched as a treatment for chronic fatigue and depression but doctors discovered it helped a lot with ADHD symptoms.

PROS OF MEDICATION

Perhaps you're already on the medication journey and you know it well enough that I can't tell you anything new. It's pretty common for parents to want to research this treatment inside and out before giving the green light. But in case you haven't journeyed down the medication path, I'll include some pros and cons so you can understand what it offers.

Not every child needs medication and most doctors will suggest behavioral therapy as a suitable treatment. That being said, medication can be really helpful for children. On medication, some children:

- Have better focus
- Fidget less
- Slow down
- Listen better
- Engage with their peers better

Medication does not cure ADHD but it can be really effective in managing the symptoms, as you can tell from the list above.

ADHD medication works by interacting with dopamine and norepinephrine. There are various kinds of medication and these are usually split into stimulants and non-stimulants. Ritalin is a brand name for a stimulant and Adderall is a well-known name for a non-stimulant.

Some of the medications can take a few weeks to start working and when they do, they can work for 24 hours. Some stimulants last around four hours, and others can last up to 12 hours. If you feel that medication would be beneficial for your child or teen, then it's worth speaking with your healthcare professional to see what might work.

One parent stated that their child started taking medication. When the father asked his son how it was going and how it was feeling, he said, "it feels like a traffic light is slowing down the cars and my ideas are arranged in a way that the light lets them pass by... Before that, it felt like the ideas and cars were chaotic and messy."

This is a beautiful vignette, describing the clarity a child can experience with the help of medication. What an amazing thing to hear! For once the ideas are lined up and the child could feel expressive and clear, without the chaos and messiness they felt before.

Take a moment to reflect on your feelings toward medication. This can be really helpful because oftentimes we don't stop to wonder about our thoughts on medication. If you have any thoughts or concerns, please talk to your healthcare professional. If your child is acting in any way concerning, you can always see what can be done to increase or decrease their medication.

CONS OF MEDICATION

With every medication, there are some downsides or disadvantages. Sometimes we take medication and it just flat out doesn't agree with us! That's okay. There are lots of alternatives on the market and there are people you can talk to about it.

For some people, there can be negative side effects when taking medication. This doesn't happen for everyone, and a lot of side effects will go away after a few days or weeks. It's important to keep in mind that some medications can take a few weeks to kick in too. If you can wait it out, it might turn out to be a positive experience overall.

Some of the side effects that can affect people taking ADHD medications include:

- Dizziness
- Nausea
- Loss of appetite
- Sleep disruption
- Headaches
- Moodiness
- Irritability

These side effects might seem really worrying or, they might seem like a good enough trade-off for management of symptoms. If you have questions, you can speak to people who have experienced ADHD medication, as well as your healthcare provider.

When you have more than one child with ADHD

ADHD runs in families. If you don't have it, maybe your husband and child do. Maybe you have a sibling with neurodivergence and multiple children diagnosed with the condition. Regardless of where it comes from, it's important to look at what the experience of having multiple children with ADHD can be like.

One thing I can say for certain is that you have your hands full. There might be double the hyperactivity, double the frustration, and double the disorganization. When there's a high level of stress and unhappiness, it's definitely worth speaking to your healthcare provider about medication. You can only manage so much on your own.

If you are struggling with a lot of emotional dysregulation in your home, you will be left drained and exhausted. Do what you need to do, in order to keep everything ticking over and running smoothly (one can dream of a smooth ride!)

Medication is definitely not for everyone. But it's a resource that can be drawn upon when things are feeling unbearable. If you need some reassurance, talk to your doctor. You can always speak your mind and try out available options.

Summing it up

Medication is a valuable resource for conditions such as ADHD. For some children, it helps slow down their chaotic thoughts in a way that makes life more doable. For others, the side effects get in the way of the benefits.

- Medication is a subjective choice and it's worth at least a conversation with your healthcare provider.
- Medication can help children engage better with peers, focus more, and stop fidgeting.
- ADHD has been around forever and the medicating of this began more than fifty years ago.

That's it for now on medication. It's a subjective decision and the take-home goal here is to feel confident in whatever decision you come to. We're going to tackle self-care and how to make your days a little easier, so you can help your child with everything they need to do.

8

A LOOK INTO THE FUTURE

"Remember to celebrate milestones as you prepare for the road ahead."

— NELSON MANDELA

You have done fantastic work so far! I can say that because I know the hard work it takes to stretch and grow into a better-equipped parent. It's not for the faint of heart! Looking into the future, what do you see for yourself and your family? Are you hoping for anything in particular? Let yourself put it down on paper and let yourself rest in the certainty that you can get yourself at least a little closer to that vision.

It's time to focus on you. You are a parent and you are doing as much as you can and when you can. Your child will need a rejuvenated parent and it's time to just visit the topic of self-care, and the positives of ADHD. There are a lot of negatives that need attention, but these topics need a look in too.

SELF CARE IS PUTTING ON YOUR OXYGEN MASK FIRST

We've all heard the term 'self-care' and we all have some sort of notion as to what it is. If you can imagine being on an airplane with a child, the most important thing to remember is that if things start heading south, you need to get your oxygen mask on first so you can then help your child. This analogy helps us to focus on our self-care as a priority.

But when we really take a look into our self-care routine, we might see an abyss where the care is supposed to be. What does self-care mean to you? Do you enjoy a bit of alone time? Do you like to get out into nature?

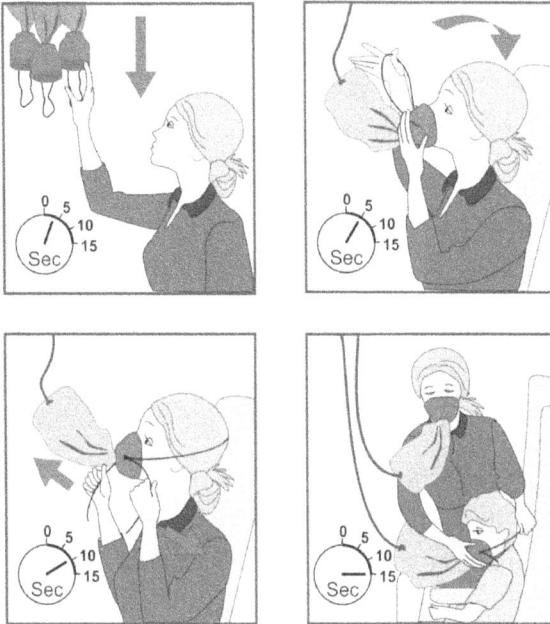

(Put on Your Oxygen Mask First: Prioritizing Self-Care, 2017)

For a lot of people, self-care means slowing down every once in a while and letting go of the things that are keeping us drained. Self-care includes:

- Putting your needs first. This is difficult when you're a parent, but it's necessary every so often. If you need some alone time and your child is trying to stay up past bedtime, be firm and put them to bed. There

might be some argument from the little one,
but you need to recharge when you can.
There will be times when you feel okay with
a late bedtime, and times when you don't.
Put your needs first when you're feeling
drained.

- Communicate what you need. If you keep
your needs locked away, you will go a long
time before they get met. Don't be afraid to
ask for help and say what you need. You will
be doing yourself and your child a disservice
by ignoring what you need.

- Make time for fun. You are important and
you were a full human before you became a
parent. Allow yourself even one night a
month to go out with friends, or one
afternoon for a fun lunch with someone who
you haven't seen in forever. You need to have
fun to keep life interesting and exciting.

- Allow yourself to make mistakes. As a
parent, you might find yourself judging your
decisions and taking mistakes really badly.
Remember that you're only human. You are
going to make some mistakes because that is
part of the human experience.

- Look after your health. This should go

without saying but a lot of parents find it hard to make doctor's appointments, or dental appointments until the situation has gotten too bad. You won't be able to take care of others if you haven't taken care of yourself, first.

- Set boundaries when you need to. Some people are used to taking up a lot of our time and resources and this can be really draining over time. If you need to set some boundaries, go for it. This is important for relationships because we can become a bit of a doormat without even realizing it, over time.

You deserve to feel happy and you deserve to have some space for yourself. When you're a parent of a child with ADHD, you need extra self-care because some days are really hard. Try to schedule your self-care until it becomes a habit you don't even need to think about.

Happy children have happy parents!

Take a look at this "wellbeing wheel" and see where you fit:

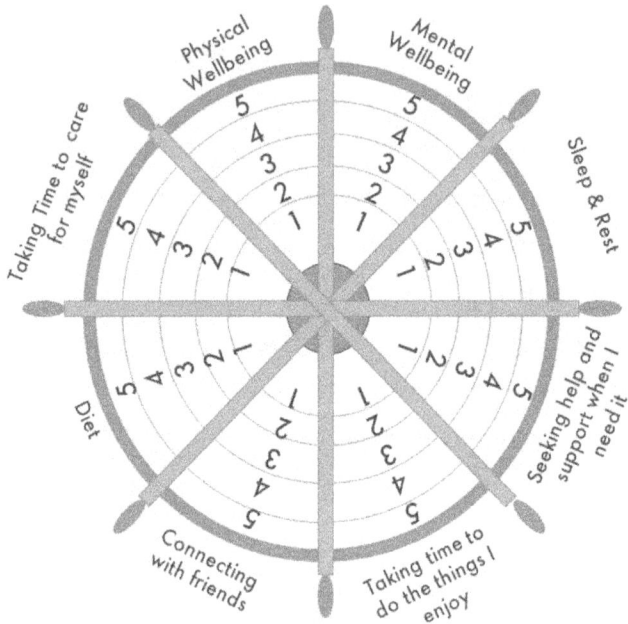

This wheel helps you assess how well you are taking care of yourself. You look at each area and rate it from one to five.

1= Very Poor; 2=Poor

3=Okay; 4=Pretty good but could be better and

5= The best you can be.

This is a really helpful tool for checking in on your self-care needs, so use it as much as possible!

Guilt about ADHD

Okay, so there's an elephant in the room we haven't said 'hello' to yet. That elephant is the blame we can take on as parents. When a child comes home with a diagnosis, we can question ourselves, our actions, and the pregnancy. We might feel like we are somehow to blame for our child's difficulties. No one is to blame when a child has ADHD.

Honestly, it's not even helpful to think like that. It's a normal reaction to a diagnosis, and it will take some time to accept. But when you accept ADHD, you can move past the worries and start to embrace your child for who they are, and help them reach their potential.

THE AMAZING ATTRIBUTES OF ADHD

There are a lot of negative things people could say about ADHD, and it's a difficult guest to welcome into your household at times. But there are so many wonderful elements of ADHD and it's important to name these.

First off, a person with ADHD has laser hyperfocus when they are engaged in a task they love. They can achieve incredible things under pressure, or in a small time frame. They can learn everything there is to know about a subject they love, and they will share everything with you if you're open.

People with ADHD are incredibly creative, especially when they have a goal-oriented task. A person with ADHD is the best person to be paired up with on a group presentation because they will put so much work and diligence into making it shine, and they are more than happy to talk about their findings.

Children and adults with ADHD are regarded as highly resilient. Resilience essentially means getting back up once you've been knocked down. For those with ADHD, they have so many setbacks and obstacles that they learn how to overcome adversity in a noticeable way.

A person with ADHD views the world in an imaginative way. They are out-of-the-box thinkers and will achieve tasks in a novel way. They are intelligent in a way that can be striking. You only have to give a riddle or funny task and the person with ADHD will have it solved.

People with ADHD are often fantastic conversationalists as they get older. They are interested in what the person is saying, and they have a lot to share too. Their hyperactivity helps them to be animated when they're speaking and this really feels engaging.

A friend with ADHD will be high energy, fun, and spontaneous. This makes them super fun to be around, and exciting company. As a parent of people with ADHD, I can confirm this point!

There are a host of celebrities who have discussed their ADHD and this is wonderful news. If someone like Michael Phelps can talk about his experience growing up, then your child can look to an Olympic athlete and say, "yeah, my brain is like his!"

Michael Phelps has won 28 Olympic Medals despite being told he would never amount to anything. This is horrible to hear, but also good to know that he was resilient enough to push past that criticism. It is great for children growing up today to know that lots of people have ADHD, and it does not hold them back from achieving their goals.

Other famous people with ADHD include:

- Simone Biles
- Justin Timberlake
- Channing Tatum
- Emma Watson
- Lisa Ling
- Bex Taylor-Klaus
- Shane Victorino
- Johnny Depp
- Terry Bradshaw
- Paris Hilton

You deserve to feel happy in your role as a parent, and your child deserves to know what will help them deal with their symptoms. They also deserve to know the wonderful skills they have, as a result of ADHD. There is a lot of brilliance that will come with that diagnosis.

CONCLUSION

"Progress is rarely a straight line. There are always bumps in the road, but you can make the choice to keep looking ahead."

— KARA GOUCHER

ADHD is a challenge. It's a road you need to travel as the parent of a child with ADHD, and, hopefully, now you feel as though you have some more information and skills to help you on your way. You are doing a fantastic job and you are doing your best to learn self-care, de-escalation strategies, how to manage expectations, and what medication can offer.

Your role as a parent is to be open to learning new things. Engaging with the material I've offered is doing that, and your child will be better for it. Take a moment to let that settle in. You are doing a great job, and you're wrestling with difficult stuff. That takes courage and I hope you can acknowledge this in yourself.

Moving forward, you have techniques that will help you deal with explosions. You also have information on medication pros and cons. If you've been waiting to make a decision on this, then maybe now you have some pointers to work from.

There will be emotional dysregulation throughout your child's life, and you can see that this will impact social interactions, academic work, and home life. Understanding why these areas are impacted will also help you understand what you can do to help alleviate stress and anxiety.

The symptoms of ADHD can take over a person's life if they have little or no support. As a parent, you have given your child time and effort. By delving into the particulars of Rejection Sensitive Dysphoria, you are gaining insight into your child's world and experience. This is a wonderful gift to yourself and your child.

At this point, it's good to reflect on your understanding of ADHD. What have you learned? What has challenged you throughout this journey? What are you excited about?

You are an agent of change and by taking time out to reflect on the journey of ADHD, you are becoming an informed and educated advocate for your child. You are making sure their voice is heard. The world needs more people who do that.

I wish you the best of luck on the road ahead. I'll see you on the other side!

"What a joy it is that the road ahead is an uphill climb. For where it leads is all the way to the top."

— RALPH MARSTON

REFERENCES

72+ Special The Road Ahead Quotes That Will Unlock Your True Potential. (n.d.). Quotlr.com. https://quotl-r.com/quotes-about-the-road-ahead

ADDitude Editors. (2016, November 28). *10 ADHD Quotes to Save for a Bad Day.* ADDitude; ADDitude Magazine. https://www.additudemag.-com/slideshows/adhd-quotes-for-a-bad-day/

Additude Editors, & Silver, L. (2021, May 10). *The ADHD Brain: Neuroscience Behind Attention Deficit Disorder.* ADDitude; ADDitude Magazine. https://www.additudemag.com/neuroscience-of-adhd-brain/#:~:text=ADHD%20brains%20have%20low%20levels

American Academy of Child and Adolescent Psychiatry. (2017, February). *ADHD & the Brain*. Aacap.org; American Academy of Child & Adolescent Psychiatry. https://www.aacap.org/AACAP/Families_and_Youth/Facts_for_Families/FFF-Guide/ADHD_and_the_Brain-121.aspx

Arky, B. (2016, February 19). *How to Help Kids With Sleepover Anxiety*. Child Mind Institute; Child Mind Institute. https://childmind.org/article/how-to-help-kids-with-sleepover-anxiety/

Carpenter Rich, E., Loo, S. K., Yang, M., Dang, J., & Smalley, S. L. (2009). Social Functioning Difficulties in ADHD: Association with PDD Risk. *Clinical Child Psychology and Psychiatry, 14*(3), 329–344. https://doi.org/10.1177/1359104508100890

Centers for Disease Control and Prevention. (2019, October 15). *Data and Statistics About ADHD | CDC*. Centers for Disease Control and Prevention; Centers for Disease Control and Prevention. https://www.cdc.gov/ncbddd/adhd/data.html#:~:text=Millions%20of%20US%20children%20have

Chatbooks. (2020, September 9). *35 Best Parenting Quotes That Perfectly Sum Up Family Life | Chatbooks*.

Chatbooks.com; Chatbooks. https://chatbooks.-com/blog/quotes-about-parenting

Dodson, W. (2020, July 29). *New Insights Into Rejection Sensitive Dysphoria*. ADDitude; ADDitude Magazine. https://www.additudemag.com/rejection-sensitive-dysphoria-adhd-emotional-dysregulation/?src=embed_link

Fujiu-Baird, P. (2022, February 24). *Emotionally based school avoidance - what to do when your child refuses to go to school*. Www.clinical-Partners.co.uk; Clinical Partners. https://www.clinical-partners.co.uk/insights-and-news/child-and-adolescent-services/item/what-to-do-when-your-child-refuses-to-go-to-school

Glasofer, D. R., & Marsh, A. (2021, July 15). *Defuse Your Anxious Thoughts With These 5 Strategies*. Verywell Mind; Verywellmind.com. https://www.very-wellmind.com/ways-to-defuse-anxious-thoughts-3863037

Gunnerson, T., & Bhandari, S. (2020, July 2). *A Brief History of ADHD*. WebMD; WebMD. https://www.webmd.com/add-adhd/adhd-history#:~:text=Today%2C%20methylphenidate%20is%20the%20stimulant

Hallowell, E. (2013, October 24). *Anger Is Important — But Only When It's Managed*. ADDitude; ADDitude Magazine. https://www.additudemag.com/anger-management-techniques-for-children-with-adhd/

Hasan, S. (2021, January 29). *ADHD Medicines (for Teens) - Nemours KidsHealth*. Kidshealth.org. https://kidshealth.org/en/teens/ritalin.html#:~:text=The%20most%20common%20side%20effects

Jacobson, R. (2016, March 1). *School Success Kit for Kids with ADHD*. Child Mind Institute; Child Mind Institute. https://childmind.org/article/school-success-kit-for-kids-with-adhd/

Kaplan, M. (2018, September 19). *Using the 80/20 Rule to Set Priorities When You Have ADHD*. A Brilliant Mess ADHD. https://www.abrilliantmessadhd.com/post/using-the-80-20-rule-to-set-priorities-when-you-have-adhd

Low, K., & Swaim, E. (2009, November 18). *Does a Teacher Blame Your Child for His ADHD Symptoms?* Verywell Mind. https://www.verywellmind.com/teacher-resistance-to-adhd-20826

Martinelli, K. (2017, January 5). *Understanding Dyslexia*. Child Mind Institute; Child Mind Institute.

https://childmind.org/article/understanding-dyslexia/

Morin, A. (n.d.). *8 Common Myths About ADHD*. Www.understood.org; understood.org. https://www.understood.org/en/articles/common-myths-about-adhd

Olivardia, R. (2016, January 29). *Dyslexia and ADHD: The Learning Disabilities Connected to ADD*. ADDitude; ADDitude Magazine. https://www.additudemag.com/adhd-dyslexia-connection/

Online Etymology Dictionary. (n.d.). *Dysphoria | Etymology, origin and meaning of dysphoria by etymonline*. Www.etymonline.com; Online Etymology Dictionary. Retrieved April 19, 2022, from https://www.etymonline.com/word/dysphoria

Pacheco, D., & Dimitriu, A. (2021, January 15). *ADHD and Sleep Problems: How Are They Related?* Www.sleepfoundation.org; Sleep Foundation. https://www.sleepfoundation.org/mental-health/adhd-and-sleep

Put On Your Oxygen Mask First: Prioritizing Self-Care. (2017, January 24). CAMPUSPEAK. https://campuspeak.com/selfcare/

Richfield, S. (2006, November 30). *Stop Bullying: School Friendships & Social Skills for ADHD Kids.* ADDitude; ADDitude Magazine. https://www.additudemag.com/stop-bullying-at-school-adhd-children/

Rodríguez, G. S. (2021, January 25). *Defusion: How to Detangle from Thoughts & Feelings.* The Psychology Group Fort Lauderdale; The Psychology Group Fort Lauderdale. https://thepsychologygroup.com/defusion/

Schuck, P. (2019, December 9). *Why Your Child's ADHD Outbursts Are So Explosive — and Isolating.* ADDitude. https://www.additudemag.com/outbursts-in-adhd-children/#:~:text=Several%20-common%20characteristics%20of%20children

ShutEye. (2020, December 12). *30 Best Sleep Well Quotes for Better Sleep and Positive Mood.* ShutEye. https://www.shuteye.ai/sleep-well-quotes/

Tartakovsky, M. (2016, May 17). *21 Tips for Raising Kids with ADHD When You Have ADHD Too.* Psych Central; PsychCentral. https://psychcentral.-com/lib/21-tips-for-raising-kids-with-adhd-when-you-have-adhd-too#1

TBS Staff. (2016, August 11). *Homeschooling: Which Model Is Right for You?* TheBestSchools.org; The Best Schools. https://thebestschools.org/magazine/homeschool-style-right/#:~:text=There%20are%20roughly%20seven%20main~:text=

The Centers for Disease Control and Prevention (CDC). (2021, September 23). *What Is ADHD?* Centers for Disease Control and Prevention; CDC. https://www.cdc.gov/ncbddd/adhd/facts.html

Ticknor, L. (2010, March 11). *When Traditional Schools Fail Your Child: How to Homeschool.* ADDitude; ADDitude Magazine. https://www.additudemag.com/home-team-advantage/

Watson, S. (2008, June 13). *Types of ADHD.* WebMD; WebMD. https://www.webmd.com/add-adhd/childhood-adhd/types-of-adhd